creative ESSENTIALS

LUCY V. HAY

WRITING DIVERSE CHARACTERS FOR FICTION, TV OR FILM

creative ESSENTIALS

First published in 2017 by Kamera Books
an imprint of Oldcastle Books,
Harpenden, Herts, UK
www.kamerabooks.com

ISBN
978-0-85730-117-8   (Print)
978-0-85730-118-5   (epub)

4 6 8 10 9 7 5 3

Typeset by Elsa Mathern in Franklin Gothic 9 pt
Printed and bound by Clays Ltd, Elcograf S.p.A.

CONTENTS

FOREWORD

One of the top screenwriters working today, Shonda Rhimes, said, 'I really hate the word "diversity". It suggests something... other. As if it is something special. Or rare.' I feel the same way as Rhimes. It strikes me as bizarre how homogenised characters and stories have become. The notion of the mainstream being for 'everyone', as in white, male, straight and able-bodied, seems foolhardy at best when we consider the numbers. Most of the world is not white; plus females make up 51% of the population. Depending on which reports you read, between 1.5% and 10% of people count themselves as part of the LGBT community in the UK, with a whopping 19% of the British population having a disability – that's nearly one in five people. Studies report similar numbers for these last two demographics in the United States and other countries.

So, where are all these untold stories? We can all no doubt name some iconic novels, movies and TV shows with diverse characters and worldviews, but they still have that quality that Rhimes hates: they're notable for *being* diverse. We live in a world where certain stories rise to the top, not necessarily for being excellent, but for being 'normal', with the rest making some kind of statement, intended or not.

These statements may make internet trolls froth at the mouth – good! – but even those who welcome progress may still inadvertently stand in its way, perhaps by putting diverse characters under greater scrutiny than 'normal' characters. Wouldn't it be great to just write a fantastic story without having to worry about labels? Absolutely, yes.

Are we there yet? Probably not.

But the good news is, stories are more diverse now than they have ever been. That long-held notion that straight, white, able-bodied males are the only 'real' characters (with all other characters representative of 'issues') is on its way out at long last. Female characters – particularly protagonists – have made up the most ground, with novels especially focusing on supposedly 'unladylike' behaviour, with TV close behind. In recent years, the floodgates have opened: writers and filmmakers have created flaws as rich and varied for female leads as for their male counterparts; BAME leads don't have to be in stories *only* about race or slavery; LGBT characters *don't* have to be in coming-out or transition stories; disabled characters don't have to appear in the same-old tired stories of loneliness and struggle, ending in suicide. Characters' differences don't have to fuel the story specifically; instead, they're part of their worldview and experiences. A subtle change, but one that makes all the difference – and can potentially lead to more three-dimensional and authentic portrayals.

Regardless of how you feel about the politics of diversity, the savvy writer knows standing out from the crowd is one of the hardest things to do as a novelist or screenwriter. Far from being a 'box-ticking' exercise, writing diverse characters is a huge skill and one that cannot be underestimated. As a showcase of one's writing talent, diverse characters who feel relevant can be the difference between opening the door, or it staying resolutely shut.

In the course of this book, I will explore not only what diversity means, but the types of characters and their various role functions, which have appeared in stories across the ages. Because storytelling is constantly in flux, I will put diverse characters and the types of story in which they appear under the microscope, with ideas for writers on how to 'flip' expected tropes and conventions to keep their work fresh and relatable. I have included quotes from various industry pros, plus their Twitter handles where appropriate; I've spoken to many more producers, actors, agents, publishers, screenwriters and novelists than the ones who have made it into these pages. I have also talked to as many people as I can who identify as being from one or more of the 'top four' diverse categories, plus more besides. Returning to Shonda Rhimes, she goes further in her dismissal of the word diversity: 'I have a different word: NORMALISING.'

So, let's do this!

Lucy V. Hay, September 2017

WHAT IS **DIVERSITY**?

'In diversity, there is beauty and there is strength.'

– Maya Angelou

DIVERSITY, A DEFINITION

'Diversity works best when you can't see forced good intention.'

– Tony Jordan, TV screenwriter and showrunner

'Diversity' is very much the watchword of the moment. It turns up again and again, especially online via headlines or social media, when it comes to discussing stories in fiction, film and TV. With various organisations, initiatives, hashtags, sites and schemes dedicated to the subject, it would seem everyone – both in audiences and in the creative industries – is talking about diversity and what can be done to include more people in more stories, both on the page and on-screen.

If you look in the dictionary, 'diversity' simply means 'a range of different things'. It has synonyms such as *array, assortment, medley, mixture, mix, miscellany, multiplicity, range* and *variety*. In applying this word to fiction, film and TV, however, it has a slightly different connotation. The 'variety' the word diversity refers to, then, will often apply to:

- Race (especially Black, Asian, Minority Ethnic – 'BAME')
- Gender
- LGBT (Lesbian, Gay, Bisexual, Transgender)
- Disability

When I mention what I call the 'top four' in this book, it's these elements I mean. I'm aware these labels aren't perfect; I've attempted to use the ones that the most people a) understand and b) like to use, as demonstrated in my research (which is, in itself, ironic in a book about diversity! Please bear with me, for the sake of clarity). There are also many other diverse characters we could explore as writers – we're making the rules of our own storyworlds, after all! – and I will mention these as we go along, too. Ready? Then let's go...

ALL ABOUT INCLUSION

'I'd like to see the UK catch up [with US TV]. For purely selfish reasons, because I think we'll make better stuff. I mean, there's diversity in drama, but there are times when you sense an air of "hope everyone's noticed what we're doing, here" hanging over it. Get past that and exploit the talent. It's what showbusiness does best.'

– Stephen Gallagher, TV showrunner and novelist (@brooligan)

If you Google 'how to write female characters' you'll see there's a plethora of books on this subject: from woman-centric stories, to breakdowns of female leads, to putting the female characters of Shakespeare and Harold Pinter under the microscope, there's plenty to choose from. Yet if you Google 'how to write diverse characters', even though you get a whopping 13+ MILLION results via blog posts and social media, at the time I was writing this book there wasn't a single published book on the subject listed on Amazon. In real terms, this could very well be the first one!

My site, www.bang2write.com, is known for its inclusive commentary on characterisation. Starting first with female characterisation, B2W snowballed relatively quickly into talking about the representation of various groups of people, including (but not limited to) race, gender (including male) and disabled people, plus my own personal interest, teenagers (especially teen parents). My Bang2writers have embraced the notion that 'real' characters are not just white, straight men, with every other demographic representative of 'issues'! Why should they be?

What's more, things are changing with audiences. There is much more demand for diverse stories, featuring diverse characters. But perception of diversity has changed to such a degree in recent years that a character's 'difference' does not have to drive the story; it can be incidental. So stories featuring gay characters do not necessarily have to be about homophobia; or black characters about racism; or disabled characters about rehabilitation. Importantly, in the best representations these differences are not there for the sake of it either – they may form part of the character's worldview, or feed into the storyworld. In short, true diversity means being inclusive, but also authentic.

WHY ARE WE TALKING ABOUT DIVERSITY?

'I found it frustrating to be offered what I thought of as stereotypical roles, so I started to write myself.'

– @ZaweAshton, actor and writer

Why we're talking about diversity is, in itself, up for discussion. Like most things related to people en masse, we can only make educated guesses at what's going on and why. In the course of my research for this book, I discovered three main threads to the debate:

1. **We NEED diverse stories.** There is a strong campaign, especially online and across a number of platforms, organisations and individuals, that suggests diverse stories actively change society and break down barriers. Campaigners will say that fiction, film and TV should reflect the world around us and even have the capacity to save lives or boost self-esteem. And how better to achieve this, these campaigners argue, than for creators to present role models who can connect marginalised people, effectively humanising and empowering them, in a world that otherwise 'others' and belittles them? Other commentators, meanwhile, say it is not

the responsibility of the creator to create positive reinforcement for marginalised people, especially when drama is conflict and antagonistic forces are necessary in creating stories. After all, we don't read or watch stories to see characters all having a jolly good time! Storytelling is not education, they counter-argue; plus stories can only go so far anyway, up against decades or even centuries of subjugation. Blame society, they say; not the writers.

Personally, and paradoxically, I think both ideas are correct. Sure, storytelling is important. I have to believe that, else I would feel like I'm wasting my life as a creator right now! So I totally get it when people respond to reflections of their own lives and worldviews in characters, because I do as well. But are we OVERestimating media images and UNDERestimating people's lived experiences? It's a chicken/egg situation so it's hard to tell, though I think it's possible the notion of positive role models and words like 'empowerment' can be red herrings. That said, I also think there's a happy medium to be had where creators can help with what I call 'intentional inclusion' – why not use one of the top four, if you can? What can writers gain? Probably a lot, especially since audiences get behind unusual characters who feel authentic and fresh. Audiences seem bored of 'the same-old, same-old'.

2. **Social media equals social change.** Some people think it's social media that has galvanised discussion of this issue and pushed it to the forefront at last. For the first time, audiences have a direct mouthpiece back to creators – especially via the likes of Facebook and Twitter – to describe the types of stories and characters they want (and possibly, and more frequently, what they *don't* want as well!). Others believe social media has made an impact in a different way, in that creators are being introduced to concepts and communities they may never have considered or come across before. This, then, has allowed them to access real people and their lived experiences, so their research is more meaningful and relevant, taking writers outside their own 'comfort zones'. Others say it's a combo of both.

There's no question growing up in the digital age has its own challenges, but others are of the opinion one huge advantage young people today have is the fact they're connected to pretty much everyone who has their own internet connection. As a result, their experiences, expectations and friendship groups reflect this. Diversity seems 'common sense'; it is not surprising, shocking or weird to them, but rather part of the natural order of things. Rightly or wrongly, I think social media has created some social change in young people. Granted, there's probably not as much as any of us would like (especially given the rise of the 'alt-right' and internet troll), plus progress is slow, too. However, I do think connection, overall, probably does create more empathy. I've also encouraged my Bang2writers to talk to people online and discovered that, nearly always, they become better at writing their stories, either directly (via research) or indirectly (in becoming more open-minded generally).

3. **Diverse stories make money!** Fiction, films and TV with diverse characters have consistently made money over a prolonged period, especially post-2010, and especially those with female leads. Properties like *The Hunger Games* have made the largest and most obvious splash, taking in novels and movie adaptations, but other female-led stories have enjoyed considerable success, not just in the young adult subgenre, either. Female characters in crime fiction have enjoyed what's known as the '*Gone Girl* Effect', with more female antagonists than ever, thanks to wicked Amy Dunne. What's more, the likes of Rachel in *The Girl on the Train* mean there are more flawed female protagonists, often with traditionally 'male' problems, such as alcoholism, but also many different depictions of mental health problems. Even in the traditionally male arena of the silver screen and blockbuster movies, we are seeing more diversity. Furiosa's robotic arm in *Mad Max: Fury Road* (2015) was singled out as not so much a disability but an 'upgrade', especially as it acts as a plot point in the story when she rescues Max when he almost falls from the

war rig. Even the female *Ghostbusters* reboot has made more money than reported, especially via ancillary markets like toys and dressing-up costumes, which little girls apparently couldn't get enough of.

I think it's probably an amalgamation of all three arguments, to a greater or lesser degree, depending on individual perception. There have been many attempts to streamline and predict audience data, some more successful than others. But notions of audience are not an exact science, with a lot of assumptions and generalisations attached. This is perhaps one reason publishers and producers are so risk averse: when they see something is working, they will continue with it, which can, in part, go some way to explaining the lack of diversity when it comes to characters in fiction, film and TV... but also why publishers and producers are becoming more willing to take a chance, too. If something 'not the norm' finds its audience, then a previously risk-averse industry is more willing to go for unusual properties. Nothing more, nothing less – and this is why the audience is so important and key in getting our diverse characters written and published or produced. I've always believed that if there's money to be made, someone will want what you can do – they don't care WHO you are. This is the downside of capitalism, to be sure, but it's also a huge opportunity, especially nowadays. The stage has been set, audiences have already proved there IS a marketplace for this stuff. All we have to do (!) is provide what people want, in a way that is true to ourselves as creators. In other words, we don't sell out, but we do SELL. It's the way forward.

POLITICAL CORRECTNESS GONE MAD?

'As a straight, white, middle-class male my tribe has long had a monopoly on characters, so it's time for people, situations and concerns I've never considered!'

– Stephen Follows, film producer (@StephenFollows)

When talking about diversity – in any field – it doesn't take long before someone utters the phrase 'It's political correctness gone mad!'. Other complaints may be that diversity is 'being rammed down our throats', or that there is a 'tick-box culture'. These same people may also make points on how quotas might not be helpful, or even make things worse (and, indeed, there is some anecdotal evidence to suggest this). They may also state a desire to be 'blind', wishing only for the 'best person (or character) for the job'.

In an ideal world, whomever is 'best' for a role should of course be the person who gets it. Yet, by this logic, looking at the world around us, in the Western world at least, whomever is 'best' is usually white, male, heterosexual and able-bodied. This doesn't make a lot of sense when there are so many talented female, BAME, LGBT and disabled people – and that's just for starters.

The reality is, we live in a diverse world, yet the majority of stories historically have featured characters who fit the white, straight, able-bodied mould. Don't believe it? In the internet age, you don't have to go far to find that someone has already crunched the numbers – multiple times, in multiple ways! Here are just a few reports and studies that have examined this issue in the past five or six years:

- In 2011, Florida State University published a study called 'One Hundred Years of Gender Bias in Children's Books'. They selected nearly 6,000 books, all written and published between 1900 and the year 2000. They discovered males are central characters in 57% of children's books published per year, while only 31% have female central characters. Shockingly, while male characters appear in 100% of the books selected, no more than 33% of children's books published in any given year contain central characters who are adult women or female animals.

- In 2014, The Geena Davis Institute on Gender in Media released a report that examined movies made between 2010 and 2013 in Australia, Brazil, China, France, Germany, India, Japan, Russia, South Korea and the United Kingdom. The report discovered there are 2.24 male characters for every female, with just 30.9% of speaking parts for female characters overall.

- The Media, Diversity and Social Change Initiative at USC's School for Communication and Journalism released a report called 'Inequality in 800 Popular Films'. It examined the fact only 2.4% of the characters in the top 100 films in 2015 had a disability. Most of these disabled characters were male, with only 19% female disabled characters. Shockingly, ALL of them were white; none had LGBT status, either.

- In 2015, the Hollywood Diversity Report from UCLA's Bunche Center estimated that leading actors (thus, the vast majority of characters) were overwhelmingly white (93%) and male (96%).

- In research commissioned by Women in Film and Television UK (WFTV UK), it was discovered females made up 29% of protagonists in 2016. Female characters accounted for 37% of all major characters in 2016. (Despite seeming rather low, these are historic highs for female characters.) These numbers fell when race was introduced: female Asian characters doubled from 3% in 2015 to 6% in 2016; black female characters increased slightly from 13% in 2015 to 14% in 2016.

- In 2016, GLAAD published its 'Where We Are on TV' report, detailing that they had found 43 LGBT characters in 895 popular primetime TV shows. Forty-three characters – that's 4.8% – were identified as gay, lesbian, bisexual, transgender and queer. This is the highest percentage of LGBT series regulars GLAAD has ever found.

Obviously these reports just scratch the surface – plus there are many more out there, too. But, overall, we can see that, ultimately, there is good news and bad news. Diversity might be increasing for female characters, but we still have a long way to go in terms of combining gender and race, for example. The incidence of LGBT characters may be at an historic high on television, but disabled characters are just as poorly represented as ever. In addition to the top four, too, there are many other characters who are not well represented, or excluded altogether. In other words, we must not get complacent. Novels, TV and films are the most diverse they have ever been, but writers, filmmakers and creators still have a long way to go.

MYTHS ABOUT DIVERSITY

'(Diverse characters) have to be more than stereotypes or ciphers; they need to have some depth, to have quirks and flaws, foibles and secret dreams.'

– **Cath Staincliffe, TV showrunner and novelist**

With all the discussion, studies, reports and roundtables on diversity in the last few years, it doesn't take long before various unhelpful myths, fallacies and incorrect assumptions emerge, especially on social media. Working with writers on their scripts and novels (or even just on their ideas and loglines), I have ended up going over the following multiple times:

- **White writers 'shouldn't' write BAME characters.** Sometimes it's floated white writers are more likely to get praise, awards, exposure and sales than BAME writers, so they should 'leave' BAME writers to tell BAME stories. Other times, the debate may centre on the notion a white writer cannot fully understand what it is like to be a person of colour or have to deal with a racial issue, as being white means being 'top of the hierarchical tree' in society. This may be backed up with evidence in the form of examples of the kind of exploitative, stereotypical or tokenistic characterisation of BAME characters that has unfortunately formed a lot of cinema, TV and novel offerings.

  B2W TAKE: While BAME and white people obviously have different heritages, which may mean different worldviews and experiences,

I still believe, as humans, we can empathise and relate to one another within certain universal parameters. As a white woman, I think it's more a question of adequate research and due diligence when writing a person of colour, just as I would a male character. In contrast, it's certainly true the industry is white-centric and a white writer – novelist or screenwriter – is more likely to get the kind of success many equally talented BAME writers only dream of. But I don't think the answer is NOT writing a BAME character, story or worldview. Instead, as a white writer, I see it as my responsibility to actively seek out and help as many BAME writers as I can. I feel this is much more likely to help BAME writers break through than censoring my own writing.

- **Men are rubbish at writing women.** Sometimes men will tell me they 'can't' write women, or fear they will make a hash of it. They may confess the female of the species seem like aliens to them in that women 'must' have had polar opposite experiences growing up or in the workforce (Note: these are not Neanderthal men, either). This feeling is echoed by women even more strongly: they may insist men 'can't' understand what it is to be a woman or girl and may cite the plethora of sexual assaults visited on female leads as 'evidence' of this.

  B2W TAKE: I've read countless spec screenplays and unpublished novels now through B2W; plus, I'm a voracious reader and die-hard movie fan. Taking into account all the good AND bad characterisation of female characters I've read and seen, plus the writers who've written them, I see NO correlation between the gender of the writer and the representation of female characters. In other words, men may write female characters well; women may write female characters badly – and vice versa. Whether you're XY or XX, it's a writer's talent – and great research – that delivers a three-dimensional, authentic female character.

- **Direct experience is necessary to write authentically.** Sometimes it is argued that the best stories and characters are drawn from the writer's direct experience. Following this logic, when writing about 'issues', the people able to produce the most potent writing and viewpoints will be those who've actually lived life through that lens. So, just as BAME stories featuring racism or slavery should be told by BAME people, women should tell stories of feminism, childbirth or female oppression; LGBT writers are best suited to telling stories of growing up gay, transitioning or homophobia; and disabled people should tell stories of what it's like to have to live with their specific disability. From there, we can draw in other elements, too: teenage parents should tell their own stories; also, working-class people, older people and so on, the idea being 'taking back control' of people's 'own' narratives.

B2W TAKE: Direct experience can be a potent and powerful tool in storytelling. If someone is so inclined to write a story about their experiences, then why not? This is a literal take on 'write what you know' and it can work, not just in autobiography, but by creating a character who is LIKE us. But what if that person with the amazing life story or viewpoint can't write well? Or what if they can, but simply don't want to write about that issue? Just as many writers feel no one 'owns' a story, I think it's just as important that writers shouldn't have certain stories forced ON them. That seems to rather make a mockery of the whole idea of diversity! ALL writers should be free to write whatever they like.

- **Writers 'shouldn't' write about certain subjects or messages/ themes.** Sometimes, marginalised groups will weigh in with various expectations, demands or campaigns when it comes to certain characterisations or storylines. We see this on social media the most, with non-writers and non-filmmakers demanding that stories fit within certain parameters or be labelled 'no good'. This is never more obvious than with feminist critique, especially the use of that problematic word 'trope' (which does not mean what lay people think it means. More about this later in the book). There are also various tests and pledges that refer to storytelling as a whole, rather than individual movies, TV shows or books. Lastly, some people may campaign against the supposed message of a book, TV show or movie, even when they haven't read or seen it. Instead, their protests will be based on ideological grounds, often with the notion attached that the writers 'shouldn't' have written about such a subject, or employed a specific message or theme. These writers may be called irresponsible, or even bad people who actively want to harm marginalised groups. Other times a campaigner may be familiar with the book, movie or TV show and even like it as an individual story, but still feel it is perpetuating certain problematic stereotypes or other issues.

B2W TAKE: I've got a certain sympathy with this viewpoint; it can be infuriating when we see a story where the writer hasn't done their due diligence, especially if we have direct experience of what is being written about. An example: Not Dead Yet, a campaign against assisted suicide for disabled people, coordinated protests against JoJo Moyes' book *Me Before You* and the subsequent movie adaptation. The plot centres on a disabled character and assisted suicide, with campaigners calling it a 'snuff' book. Yet *Me Before You* has sold five million copies since its publication in 2012 and been translated into over 40 languages. More importantly, it has a 4.28 out of a possible five stars, with 678,000 ratings and 69,000 reviews on Goodreads, so the book obviously resonates with readers (some of whom will presumably be disabled themselves). As a direct result of the furore, I read the book and was surprised at how measured and nuanced it was, considering assisted suicide is such a controversial topic. Perhaps the problem is not the individual book so much, but more that disabled characters are too often in storylines like this? Katie Newstead is a PhD film studies student, archivist and researcher at Exeter University; she is also disabled herself. 'I love *Me Before You*, but we've still got a story in which a disabled man wants to die,' says Katie. 'Why can't we have a fictional paraplegic who doesn't want to die, for a change??'

Rounding up this section, then, it should be pretty obvious where I fall in the 'diverse characters' and storytelling debate… *Anyone* can write *anything* – as long as they do it justice!! What this means will, of course, depend on various things. But as Vinay Patel, screenwriter of BBC3's controversial and powerful *Murdered by My Father*, points out: 'Any writer – white, black or Asian – can write whatever they want… but the bar of responsibility is high when you're writing someone unlike yourself. Due diligence is key, which is hopefully a standard of research and care one would apply to their characters anyway.'

POSITIVE DISCRIMINATION VERSUS INTENTIONAL INCLUSION

'I'm half Middle Eastern so I regularly find myself going up for the roles of wives of terrorists or women in arranged marriages. I think where it's done well is when the character isn't all about their race.'

– **L, actress and blogger, 'Casting Call Woe' (@ProResting)**

Sometimes called 'affirmative action', positive discrimination is defined as the practice of favouring individuals belonging to groups that suffer discrimination. In real life, some people object to positive discrimination in the workplace because they say it's 'not fair' that an otherwise 'underqualified' candidate gets through on the basis of their diversity in terms of gender, race, disability, etc. Other people argue we live in a hierarchy and that it's not fair those hierarchies are set up to favour the non-diverse, so the least we can do is try to redress the balance a bit. (I'm simplifying, obviously.)

When dealing with diverse characters, however, these people are not real. You do not have to worry about their feelings or prospects, whether you do or don't pick them for your story. At foundation level, all that should concern you is the story (even if you're a screenwriter – casting should be an issue much further down the road). So, to avoid picking diverse characters for the sake of it, think about what's best for the story. Be intentionally inclusive, considering how diverse characters could work, rather than ticking boxes via 'positive discrimination'.

DIVERSITY IN THE PRESENT

'A lot of people focus on diverse fiction being "stories about diversity" when it should be "stories that are diverse". Diversity needs to be normalised. A diverse story shouldn't also have to be "A Unique Original Event About It"!'

– Olivia White, games developer (@owlcavedev)

Though the issue of diversity has never 'gone away', there have been a number of very high-profile furores regarding diversity in the last few years, covering fiction, TV and film, including (but not limited to):

- **Male authors vs female authors.** With frightening regularity, it's discovered male authors dominate the literary world. Men are more likely to get critical acclaim, with some readers even confessing to 'preferring' books by men. The blogosphere was set alight in 2015 when writer Catherine Nichols discovered she got EIGHT TIMES as many responses from literary agents when she submitted the same book as a man.

- **LGBT inclusion.** Two prominent, award-winning movies, *Dallas Buyers Club* (2013) and *The Danish Girl* (2015), had straight male actors playing trans women, which created an outcry among some groups, especially online. There was also a lot of commentary about the lack of BAME/LGBT talent/stories, with many showing up for *Moonlight* (2016), which won the Academy Award for Best Picture in 2017.

- **'Whitewashing' of Asian characters in adaptations.** Despite being East Asian in the source material, The Ancient One is played by Tilda Swinton in *Doctor Strange* (2016); plus The Major is played by the very white Scarlett Johansson in 2017's *Ghost in the Shell*. Though the casting of white stars in BAME roles is common, these two properties are so iconic they really grabbed the headlines.

- **Disability inclusion.** 'Diversity' was most often thought to include gender, race and LGBT status, but 2016 marked the year disability finally became part of the conversation. There were more articles and column inches devoted to disabled representation in creative works, plus events like the Ruderman Studio-Wide Roundtable on Disability Inclusion, held by the Ruderman Family Foundation, helped create even more. Oscar-winning actress Marlee Matlin, who is deaf, led the call for more disabled inclusion in Hollywood.

- **BAFTA.** In December 2016, it was announced that, as of 2019, BAFTA will no longer consider films for some of its awards if they are considered 'non-diverse'. To be eligible, films must prove they have worked to improve diversity in two of the four following areas: on-screen characters and themes; senior roles and crew; industry training and career progression; and audience access and appeal to underrepresented audiences. This was warmly accepted by many in the creative industries, though, inevitably, BAFTA was accused of 'box ticking' by some.

- *Ghostbusters.* The 1984 classic was remade in 2016 with an all-female cast. Cue a gazillion 30- and 40-somethings insisting their childhoods had been 'ruined' by so-called 'studio cash grabs'! Some commentators even suggested women could not be as funny as the original actors; or that having an all-female cast was some sort of automatic political statement. Alt-right hero Milo Yiannopoulos was eventually banned from Twitter after he and his followers tried to drive one of the movie's stars, Leslie Jones, offline with racist and misogynistic attacks. Regardless, the movie received a 'Fresh' rating from critics via reviews aggregator site Rotten Tomatoes and there's apparently a sequel in the works.

- **Lionel Shriver.** The award-winning author made a scathing speech about diversity in fiction at the Brisbane Writers Festival on what she termed 'cultural appropriation and identity politics'. Not sure what this is? Don't worry – the short version of Shriver's speech is basically 'it's political correctness gone mad!'.

- **#OscarsSoWhite.** Despite a Best Picture win and sweeping of the board for *12 Years a Slave* in 2013, there was a dearth of BAME nominees in subsequent years. The call to arms was raised by April Reign, editor of theatre blog *Broadway Black* and key spokesperson for 'Black Twitter', which in itself has become a powerful commentator on race and gender in the social media landscape. As 2017 was radically different in terms of nominations, many credit #OscarsSoWhite as having played a fundamental part in that change.

This is just a small selection of the headlines in the last couple of years. But you get it: diversity is the 'thing of the moment', so the savvy writer would do well to pay attention.

DIVERSITY IN THE PAST

'Sometimes the point of a story is to tell it from a specific and particular point of view. Is one POV used more than others? Yes. Should there be more variety? Also yes.'

– Toby Forrest, runner at the BBC (@Tobiiiaaas)

While the spotlight might be on diversity right now, in real terms it is nothing new when it comes to creative works. There have always been writers and creators who have striven to tell diverse stories and/or bring marginalised voices and characters to the fore. Some of these efforts have worked well, others less so, often dependent on the context of attitudes and beliefs of the time. If we consider a character like Shylock in William Shakespeare's *The Merchant of Venice*, modern audiences most likely consider him a grotesque stereotype of a Jewish money-lender. There is plenty of evidence to support this. Shylock, on the surface at least, is greedy and driven by hatred, keen on getting his literal pound of flesh because, really, he hates Antonio. He is a comic-book villain, designed to give Jacobean audiences a focus for their own prejudices. (This is why people so often make the mistake of viewing antagonists as personifications of the writer's own bigotry – sometimes it seems irrefutable.)

Yet is Shylock really as two-dimensional as he appears on the page, especially when his portrayal is in language we no longer use daily, or relate to that well? There have been many compassionate portrayals of Shylock in the 450-odd years since he was written. This is no doubt inspired by his famous and rousing speech, where he argues that he is, in fact, a human being, just like Antonio and the rest of his cronies: 'Hath not a Jew eyes? Hath not a Jew hands, organs, dimensions, senses, affections, passions; fed with the same food, hurt with the same weapons, subject to the same diseases, healed by the same means, warmed and cooled by the same winter and summer as a Christian is? If you prick us, do we not bleed?'

Keeping with Shakespeare and the various adaptations of his work, let's turn to a seemingly forgotten collaboration between a 19-year-old Orson Welles and New York's Negro Theatre Unit: 'Voodoo Macbeth', brought to the stage in 1936. Transposing the play's storyworld to Haiti, and featuring an all-black cast and performed in front of a segregated audience, it was so popular its initial run was extended. If you Google 'Voodoo Macbeth' you can find four minutes of footage of this extraordinary production, with its voiceover artist claiming 'the spirit of Macbeth and every line of the play has remained intact'.

As with any risk-taking and diverse project, critical opinion was sharply divided. Some, including those in the black community, claimed it was 'racist comedy'. Other notable black figures were pleased black actors' talents were on display. We see this type of discussion to this day, especially online via Twitter. Writers often confess to feeling 'worried' about including diverse characters in their novels and screenplays in case they upset someone like this. I always counsel them with:

- You cannot please everyone, especially within a certain community. You can only do your research and be as authentic as possible.

- Twitter is always angry about something, so it might as well be your work.

- You have to get published or produced FIRST before worrying about this!

Writers get paralysed by the audience's expectations sometimes. In today's 'call-out' culture online, a lot of assumptions get made about creators' intentions and motivations, or how much research they have done. It's also a sad fact that the more diverse characters tend to get the greater scrutiny; sometimes writers and creators will get called all kinds of names for simply telling a story! When this happens, you must withdraw. It's not a real debate, nor even an argument that can be won – the accusers have decided what you have done. Every successful writer gets this. Honest! But also, like I say, you have to get there first. As the old saying goes, 'cross that bridge when you come to it'.

WHAT IS 'GOOD' CHARACTERISATION?

'As with all characters, give them flaws and complications. Not necessarily to do with their gender, sexuality, race or disabilities. Make sure they have concerns outside of that. Let them love, hate and rage.'

– Lisa Holdsworth, screenwriter and playwright (@WorksWithWords)

There is a huge ongoing discussion among writers about what constitutes 'good' characterisation, which usually centres around the notion of character 'arc'. Unhelpfully, what a character arc entails is different to different people. However, a writer does not have to go far to discover that the main component of this debate is usually about whether characters 'change'… or not. In today's writing world, the argument usually breaks down something like this:

- **Good characters always change.** These writers will insist on what I call the 'transformative arc'… in other words, characters will learn something or come to some kind of important realisation about themselves, the world and/or life by the end of the narrative. It's not difficult to see why writers believe this: the majority of narratives carry a 'transformative arc', especially for the protagonist. They will be changed in some way by their journey through the story. It's thought that if a character does not change, it is 'bad' characterisation.

- **Good characters don't have to change.** These writers will point to different types of protagonist, such as the 'Change Agent'. This character does not change, but instead inspires change in all the other characters around him. A classic example of this type of protagonist would be Forrest Gump, who remains the same throughout his story journey; we see change in the story via other characters like Lieutenant Dan, who goes from pride to despair to a new way of looking at the world. These writers may say there is no such thing as 'bad' characterisation, just different ways of looking at it.

- **It depends on the story and what it needs to do.** As ever, I believe there is a happy medium to be had on this issue. While it's true the majority of stories have a 'transformative arc' for their lead characters, this is not the only way forward. There are lots of other advanced character techniques, like the Change Agent, writers can exploit (and should, if they want to write more diverse characters). In addition, it's possible to write a more traditional protagonist who doesn't change, too. I have always argued that Ellen Ripley from *Alien* (1979) does not have a 'transformative arc'. Intriguingly, whenever I posit this, writers will insist she does change, as though to say otherwise makes Ripley a 'bad' character. But I say she is refreshingly consistent: Ripley starts and ends the movie as someone who knows her own mind and will do whatever it takes, whether that is running the *Nostromo* as second officer or surviving the attack of an acid-dripping alien. She has no tragic backstory to 'get over' in the course of that either – because isn't a hostile alien on board enough??

Science-fiction author Veronica Sicoe (@veronicasicoe) writes of character arc in a way I can get behind. She describes character arc as having three main types: 'Growth' (the classic idea of change or transformation); 'Shift' (where a protagonist will need to shift his or her perspective, somehow via a different role, with different skills) (Note: the end result here is not 'better', just different); and 'Fall' (usually associated with tragedy, our protagonist will end up leading the bad guys, or signing his/her own death warrant somehow). I would say, then, that Ripley has a 'Shift' arc – after all, even once she escapes the creature on board the *Nostromo*, her life will never be the same again as she leads expedition after expedition against the Xenomorph in the franchise.

WHAT IS 'BAD' CHARACTERISATION?

'Easier to say what I hate! Like characters too stupid to live, doing something no sane person would do, such as entering a room/ cave/dark without a torch, or not calling the police when they need to! I also hate perfect characters... no one is perfect.'

– Liz Fenwick, author (@Liz_Fenwick)

While there are favourite characters 'everyone' seems to like, just like favourite stories, these will always have their detractors as well. Some of these complaints will be valid; others not so much. Most will hover somewhere in the middle. What's more, there will be just as many – if not more! – people who have no clue who that character is. Human beings are individuals and consume and perceive stories according to their personal worldviews, experiences and understanding. On this basis, there cannot ever be one universal character or story that is for 'everyone'. There is no such thing. Perhaps inevitably, it's easier to describe what bad characterisation is than good:

• Bad characterisation feels two-dimensional, wooden, unbelievable and inauthentic

- Characters feel clichéd and make use of stale, overused and even offensive tropes
- Characters don't feel relatable, or relevant to the reader or audience
- They feel like stock characters or stereotypes
- There are 'too many' characters, so readers and viewers can't keep track of who is doing what and why in the story
- Characters feel 'tick box' – like the writer has lifted them straight from another work, or to satisfy an agenda or soapbox of their own
- Characters feel like plot devices, there solely to go through the motions
- Characters have boring goals we've seen a million times before
- Characters don't have clear motivations – we don't know what the protagonist wants or why the antagonist wants to stop them (or similar)
- Characters don't have clear role functions – we don't know who the protagonist or antagonist are, or why the secondary characters are there

Taking all this into account, WHO your character is, WHAT they are doing in the story and WHY they are doing it is key in ensuring your readers or viewers get onboard with your story – whether you're attempting diversity or not.

RELATABILITY AND RELEVANCE

'I like characters who are different to the norm but ones I can identify with on some level. Ideally, I'd like more characters that challenge me and initially throw me out of my comfort zone, only to draw me closer to them as I get to know their stories.'

– Mark Renshaw, screenwriter (@markyrenshaw)

'Relatable' and 'relatability' – as well as hashtags and sayings like #relatablemuch – are modern words that have sprung up in the social media age. These are words young people may use a lot, which us 'grown-ups' may complain about! But writers should ignore 'relatable' and its many versions at their peril, because it is 'relatability' that enables us to find our target audience, because when someone says a character or story is 'relatable', what they're saying is that the character or story feels RELEVANT. This is the 'Holy Grail' when it comes to creative writing, because relevance means people will WANT IT.

First, though, a short history. In the past, much has been made of 'likeable' characters in writing classes, books and by so-called 'gurus'. The notion that an audience has to actively LIKE the protagonists whose journeys, missions or problems they are reading or watching is understandable on the surface – after all, who wants to watch the story of an evil despot who tries to take over the world? Oh, quite a lot of people it turns out! Some of the most iconic characters are antagonists, with evil plans: Darth Vader in the *Star Wars* franchise and Lord Voldemort in the *Harry Potter* series are the most obvious, but there are lots of others.

So 'likeable' was swapped for 'sympathetic' or 'empathetic'. But, again, these words fell short. Antagonists are frequently just as popular as protagonists, if not more so, especially in stories with a thriller element. In addition, the phenomenon of so-called 'anti-heroes' means the protagonist can be badly behaved, yet still earn our interest and even love. There is nothing remotely 'sympathetic' or 'empathetic' about the likes of Melvin Udall in *As Good as It Gets* (1998), who is both a misogynist and a homophobe; or the generally misanthropic Walt Kowalski in *Gran Torino* (2008) or Riddick in *Pitch Black* (2000), who is a murderer and manipulator.

Instead, audiences relate to these characters: who hasn't met a disgruntled, angry old man like Udall or Kowalski? We feel sorry for the latter and are impressed by the former, who is so outrageous, we can't wait to see what he says next. Riddick, in comparison, is a subtle twist on the classic muscle-bound hero, on every level: he's not anyone's saviour, he's not even white. Instead, he's dangerous, out for what he can get – in effect, the exact opposite of what audiences in the sci-fi/action/thriller genre expect. It's no wonder Riddick was a star-making turn for Vin Diesel (just a shame they weren't able to capture lightning in the bottle for the subsequent two sequels).

It is easy to say words like 'role models', 'empowerment' or 'postive representation' when talking about diversity in storytelling. It is also understandable that writers may feel the responsibility to do this, or that audiences may think they want it. And in some stories, this is desirable. However, it's important to note that true diversity means bad characters, too, warts and all. An antagonist is just a role function, not a moral judgement; it might seem that way when 'bad' characters are 'all the same' – but that is why we need diversity. More on this, next.

DRAMA = CONFLICT

'Positive representation is great. But flawed characters are more interesting, believable and can be invested in more.'

– Robin Bell, screenwriter and filmmaker (@robinbellwriter)

When drama is conflict, it's also perfectly possibly to be in awe of, or even enjoy, a character's bad behaviour, while not condoning it. One of the biggest controversies surrounding Gillian Flynn's *Gone Girl* was Amy Dunne's appalling use of violence against women in her own favour. At various points in the story, she pretends to be a battered wife, rape survivor and kidnap victim. As a character, Amy Dunne is, without a doubt, a truly horrific human being. Flynn was accused of misogyny AND misandry in penning both the novel and the movie (no mean feat!).

But Amy Dunne is an embodiment of what some *infamous* women in real life have done: knowing the law often sees women as victims, certain women have played on this assumption to take down husbands, boyfriends, brothers and work colleagues in high-profile cases. One such case that comes to mind is that of Karla Homolka, one half of the 'Ken and Barbie Killers' in Toronto in the nineties. She and her husband, Paul Bernardo, were convicted of the rape and murder of at least three young women, including Karla's own teenage sister, Tammy. During her trial Homolka insisted she had been under the manipulative influence of her husband, a claim many psychology and law experts believe was accepted because Homolka was female and Bernardo was male. Later it was revealed this was a lie, with Homolka using society's narrative of 'women as victims' to her own advantage. But by then it was far too late: Homolka's plea bargain, plus her resulting more lenient sentence, was in place and the blame had been laid squarely at Bernardo's door.

So, it's this word, 'relatability', that enabled the success of *Gone Girl*. There's literally nothing Amy Dunne won't do to get what she wants, which is revenge on her feckless, unfaithful husband, Nick. Flynn takes the classic notion of 'Hell hath no fury like a woman scorned' and runs with it, asking what WOULDN'T you do, to get your revenge on a cheating spouse? The notion of 'being traded in for a younger model' is something the women in the audience may be terrified of, perhaps having seen it in their own families as fathers or brothers-in-law leave their mothers and sisters. But betrayal and infidelity can bite deep and the scars last for years, regardless of gender, so who wouldn't want to get even? While not all of us would seek revenge, I think most people would admit to at least thinking about it, even if it's just fantasy.

As author Kirsten Lamb (@KirstenLambTX) points out, 'Great fiction is fuelled by bad decisions and human weakness.' *Gone Girl* builds on this, playing on deeply engrained gender roles and other social elements that both men and women in the target audience recognise instantly. You don't have to be trapped in a bad marriage to appreciate the irony of how the tables are turned on Nick, again and again. Every trap Amy lays, he falls into, hook, line and sinker. And we – the target audience, anyway – love it. Not because it's a 'nice' or 'positive' story – spoiler alert: every character ends up pretty much screwed over! – but because, IF you like that sort of thing, *Gone Girl* is dark, delicious and damn entertaining.

THE 'HIGHLANDER EFFECT'

'Stale character tropes... Two-dimensional characters, especially BAME ones, as if that one characteristic was enough!'

– Julian Friedmann, literary agent (@julianfriedmann)

You may recall the catchphrase 'There can be only one!' from the movie *Highlander* (1985). I relate this to diverse characters because too often they suffer what I call the 'Highlander Effect', in that such a character may be included... but there will be ONLY ONE. The rest in the cast will be default white, straight and, too often, male as well. While this may not seem like that big an issue, it does mean we end up with the following 'tick-box' characters, especially when there's teamwork or an ensemble involved:

- **The Girl Character (aka Kick-ass Hottie).** When there's a team involved, you can bet your bottom dollar there's a bunch of diverse men on it, with lots of different personalities and skills, but the ONE female is beautiful, white and sexy. However, she's just as good as any man on the fighting front and may be considered cold, or an ice maiden.

- **The Black Dude.** He's cool and NOT calm and NOT cooperative. In fact, he's mouthy and a troublemaker, but he is HILARIOUS. (<u>Note:</u> Black Dude may be swapped out for Kick-ass East Asian, occasionally. KEA is most often a martial artist and completely impassive, so the rest of the group may express disquiet at being around him.)

- **Gay Airhead.** Like the Girl Character, Gay Airhead's sexuality comes first and foremost in his characterisation. In strong contrast to Girl Character, he's feminine – which means he is less capable than the others in the team. He may make mistakes and/or need rescuing, especially by Girl Character.

- **Disabled Genius.** Most likely a wheelchair user, sometimes a person with autism, this character usually stays in the lab or headquarters. He may have to sort stuff out from afar, plus there is a stronger than average chance he'll need rescuing when he ends up captured by the antagonist (if he doesn't reveal himself as the antagonist and Behind It All Along).

Obviously, these are all grossly simplified, but we've ALL seen characters like this, especially in movies and returning drama series, but some novels, too. I read them all the time in spec screenplays, especially Girl Character and Black Dude. When people complain about diversity, they're usually thinking about this version of it... which, of course, no one wants. We want authentic, three-dimensional characters who 'feel' real, no matter how outlandish they may be.

CONNECTIONS

'I want writers of indie films to explore and delve further than in mainstream offerings. Go boldly where the studios fear to tread.'
– Steve LaRue, Hollywood producer (@SteveLaRue2)

It is important to note that 'diversity' does not just apply to the top four exclusively of one another. Any or even all of these four may cross over or intersect, within one character journey or a whole cast's. Let's consider three movies that are i) true stories, ii) deal with mathematicians and their inventions, plus iii) personal struggle:

- **Mental Health/Disability –** *A Beautiful Mind* **(2001).** The story of John Forbes Nash, a mathematician and genius who won the Nobel Prize for Economics; he also suffered from paranoid schizophrenia.

- **Mental Health/LGBT –** *The Imitation Game* **(2014).** A biopic about Alan Turing, who created the machine that cracked the Nazis' Enigma Code; he also was a homosexual in a time it was forbidden and may have been autistic.

- **Race/Gender –** *Hidden Figures* **(2016).** The story of three black, female mathematicians – Katherine Johnson, Dorothy Vaughn and Mary Jackson – who calculated trajectories for the 1969 Apollo 11 flight to the Moon.

All three of these movies follow similar paths in terms of subject matter and the characters within them, taking on marginalised people's stories and creating inspirational dramas. As far as strategies go, this is one that has been seen to work, over and over again, not only in terms of critical acclaim and winning awards, but also box-office success.

Put simply, audiences actively like true stories about real people, whose struggles feel relevant to their own. This doesn't mean audiences have to be the same as the characters in specific ways (though this can help); rather, they may take onboard the inspirational message and feel that 'If (they) can do "it", so can I'. Margot Lee Shetterly, the writer of the book *Hidden Figures* is adapted from, is spot-on when she writes: 'What I wanted was for [Katherine Johnson, Dorothy Vaughn and Mary Jackson] to have the grand, sweeping narrative they deserved, the kind of American history that belongs to the Wright brothers and the astronauts, to Alexander Hamilton and Martin Luther King Jr. Not at the margins, but at the very centre, the protagonists of the drama. And not just because they are black, or because they are women, but because they are part of the American epic.'

MORE IDEAS FOR DIVERSITY

'Humour is underrated in making characters relatable. We warm to funny characters much faster, even if they do bad things.'

– Eddie Robson, TV and radio writer (@EddieRobson)

In addition to the top four, there are many other diverse characters worth considering, such as (but not limited to):

- **Age.** Though a medium or genre may have more variety than others, the vast majority of characters we see in fiction, film and TV are still in their twenties and thirties. What about children?

Teenagers? The middle-aged? The elderly? Some ages are mandatory within certain categories – it wouldn't make much sense to have an adult protagonist in a young adult ('YA') novel, for example – but there is usually more leeway than a writer supposes, if the story is considered good enough.

- **Class.** A large proportion of British TV characters may be middle-to-working class (think soap operas) or upper class (think the likes of period drama). A large amount of novels – especially YA, crime fiction/mystery and romance – may have characters who are what British tabloids like to call 'the squeezed middle' – in other words, working people with a moderate or even high amount of education, who are still struggling to get by financially. Films seem to be more of a 'free for all' when it comes to class, which I always find interesting. If someone put a gun to my head, I'd probably say British films are more 'working class' – I'm thinking Ken Loach here – with the vast majority of American films leaning more towards the middle.

- **Religion.** Various religions may have particular practices or elements people 'outside' them find interesting, useful or even barbaric. Since drama is conflict, it's frequently the latter that's utilised – in all stories, regardless of medium. Yet it's possible to have a more nuanced approach than to make every non-white antagonist a monster. In the 2017 novel *The Marsh King's Daughter* by Karen Dionne, she creates a Native American antagonist in protagonist Helena's father. This is interesting, because immediately Jacob is at odds with Dionne's thirty-something audience's stereotypical perception of Native Americans, probably absorbed from playing games like 'Cowboys and Indians', or watching the likes of *Dances with Wolves* (1990) while growing up. Instead, Jacob is both a spiritual man AND a vicious psychopath; and what's more, his sadism never has anything to do with his heritage, but his own narcissism. This, plus Helena's tendency towards moral relativism, helps us understand Jacob's choices, without ever condoning them.

- **Country.** Regardless of the medium, 'foreign' characters will frequently seem strange or at odds with their surroundings. This is not inauthentic, as any one of us may seem strange when placed in an environment not our own. However, there are various ideas that seem synonymous with 'being foreign'. This often relates to specific political feelings of the moment. In 2017, to be a Russian male character is to be SINISTER, which is probably due to various political shenanigans. We are seeing countless Russian or Eastern European henchmen in Hollywood at the moment, especially in action movies like *Batman Vs Superman: Dawn of Justice* (2016) or the *Mission Impossible* franchise. Compare this to nearly 20 years ago, with characters such as Serge in *Armageddon* (1998), where he seems pretty comical. Had Serge been written at the height of the Cold War some 10 or 15 years before THAT, he'd probably have been represented as rather sinister again. Now compare Eastern European male characters with Eastern European female characters, who are frequently cast as the victims of human trafficking and/or exploitation, especially in TV dramas like the BBC's *Happy Valley* or soap operas like ITV's *Coronation Street*. A huge difference.

Again, I'm just scratching the surface here. There are any number of 'expected' character roles we see all the time. Some make us angry, especially if we feel these roles have been depicted in a stereotypical, clichéd or offensive manner – or when certain groups of people are excluded altogether. Other representations of certain characters may make us weary, because we see them too much: from the typical White Saviour hero narrative, through to disfigured characters who are also evil; teenage mothers who are stupid or conniving; or black men who are drug dealers... or the chief of police. This is 'either/or' mentality, and swinging from one end of the pendulum to the other can feel tedious and unnecessary, which is why so many people, both creator and audience member alike, want to see more variety in characterisation.

HITTING THE TARGET

'I'm an agent. My first thought is: can I sell this? So, obviously, that informs my opinion.'

– Oli Munson, literary agent (@oliagent)

If writers are to sell their novels and screenplays (diverse or not) to publishers and producers, they need to know who their target audience is. Unless you are a hobby writer, there is literally no point in only writing for oneself or claiming your story is for 'everyone'. No story on Earth is for everyone! This is a fact. Even a story with a mass audience, which has become so popular it's been remade, rebooted and translated into multiple languages, is *still* not for everyone. Consider these titles:

- Have you seen *Alien* (1979)? Not any of the sequels or reboots – I mean the original movie starring Sigourney Weaver. If you're over 35, you probably have. If you're under 35, you probably haven't.

- Have you seen the *Total Recall* (2012) or *Poltergeist* (2015) remakes? If you watched them first time around, it's probably 50/50 whether you have or not. Curiosity may have got you through the door, or familiarity with the originals may have made you stay away. If you weren't born the first time they came out – and enjoy action/adventure or supernatural horror – you probably have seen these remakes.

- Have you read any of the *Harry Potter* series? If you're in your early twenties, you probably have. If you've been a parent in the last two decades, you've probably read at least one of them. If you were an adult BEFORE the Harry Potter phenomenon took off and remained child-free, you may have only seen the movie adaptations, or missed them altogether.

- Have you read any of the *Twilight* saga? If you were a teen girl in the last 10 or 15 years, you probably have. You will probably have seen all the movies, too. While not many teen boys will admit to reading *Twilight*, a larger-than-you'd-think proportion of them will have watched the movies, not just because they've watched them with girlfriends, but also because *Twilight* has a devoted gay male following, especially those designated 'tweens' (roughly those between 11 and 14 years old).

These are all properties that have had HUGE audiences and continue to make good money years, or even decades, after their release. But note how I write 'probably' when I consider things like race, gender, age or status. When it comes to audiences, we're talking about people en masse again – and the tricky thing with groups of people is that they're made up of individuals!

IN A NUTSHELL: There are target audiences, with others outside these considered 'bonus' audiences. Sometimes it makes sense to target the 'usual' audience. However, some marginalised audiences are wildly underserved, so if you can find a story and target it accordingly, you may find a niche in the market and hit the bull's eye.

FINDING YOUR TARGET AUDIENCE

'The characters let us into their hearts; each one has some kind of emotional pull. We understand them; we feel their pain, their joys, their highs and lows. They "work" for the reader because they are people first, rather than some stereotyped character out to prove a point.'

– Wendy Storer, author

Some writers may accept they need a target audience, but throw their hands up in the air and ask how they are supposed to know what people want. Certainly, before the internet it was much more difficult, but there have always been ways of finding the types of stories audiences respond to (which means the industry will be looking for them!):

- **Check out all the bestselling/most downloaded/most watched lists.** Bestselling fiction, film and TV is handily listed online and in the trades. If it sells well, the industry will want more of it. Equally, if there is a type of story that's NOT selling well, the industry won't want it. Simple. That's not to say you should ONLY write what's selling, because, again, that would make you a hack. However, forewarned is forearmed and knowing if your story and/ or characters are popular – or not – WILL help you in your journey to find your target audience and get your work out there.

  IN A NUTSHELL: Contrary to popular belief among writers and creators, audiences are not invisible! We can see which properties they engaged with by looking at the ones they bought (or not).

- **Immerse yourself in <u>your</u> type of story, no matter the medium.** Whether you're writing a novel or screenplay, check out ALL the stories and characters 'like' yours across all mediums, not just recently but over the last 20 or 30 years at least. See what's changed over the decades, what's similar and what's very different. If you can, work out what's missing from them in terms of characters – because there's a strong chance that might be the character people would love to see.

  IN A NUTSHELL: You can't break new ground without knowing what has gone before.

- **Talk to people.** Discover what people would love to see and read in their favourite genres and types of story. Never turn down the opportunity to hear what people THINK they want. Now, they might be wrong, but that's interesting in itself. Overall, though, this is a way of doing informal surveys and you will discover there are many interesting ideas people have that may spark your creative juices. DO stay away from 'hate-readers' and 'hate-watchers': these are bizarre people who read stuff specifically to slag it off on social media! (They must have too much time on their hands.) Stay away from 'thinkpieces' as well – these are too often journalist hacks ranting randomly for a pay cheque about books, movies and TV shows they haven't even read or watched.

IN A NUTSHELL: Informal surveys of what people want or would love to see can only help you. Just stay away from those who get negative satisfaction from slagging stories off for the sake of it. You'll soon find out who these people are, especially online!

- **Check out trending topics and popular themes and ideas 'of the moment'.** If something seems relevant and authentic, people will generally be interested in it, whether it's intended for a niche or mass audience (or something in-between). So pay attention to the concerns and interests of society, as well as how things change, not just regarding race, gender, etc., but also in things like technology, science, politics and so on. We live in a melting-pot world, so utilising this in your characters and stories is a no-brainer.

IN A NUTSHELL: Be well informed and interested in other people. It doesn't matter how you do this, but thinking audiences are stupid is a one-way ticket to failure.

- **Find, follow and converse with the people with their fingers on the pulse.** Social media means every writer has potential access to industry pros, but there are also many events in the calendar year-round that mean you can hear the types of characters, stories and themes the industry is interested in and actively looking for. Literary agents in particular will be very clear about the types of characters and stories they are interested in. Online, Twitter events like #pitmad ('pitching madness') happen monthly for various genres, plus some agents use the #askagent and #mswl ('manuscript wish list') hashtags, too. Some producers and filmmakers, both big and small, will share their opinions and discuss how they see the industry and what audiences want. Other people – like script editors and readers such as B2W – will share what they see on a regular basis 'behind the scenes'. My personal favourite is Stephen Follows (www.stephenfollows.com), who has put everything under the microscope, from women in film, through to what older audiences are watching, plus movies based on true stories and beyond.

IN A NUTSHELL: Meet as many industry pros as you can, in real life or online – preferably both – but whatever you do, don't harangue or pitch AT them. Learn from them and create those all-important relationships.

Again – being aware of these things does NOT mean you're writing 'for' the marketplace. It doesn't have to be either/or! Unless you actually want to be a hobby writer, selling does not have to mean 'selling out'. Finding out what other people are interested in really helps you inform your own stories and get your creativity going, IF you know your target audience and what they want, or feel they are missing.

ALL ABOUT HYPE

'I don't really care about "diverse" characters – I just care about characters, period, no matter what their gender, race or sexual identity. All I care about is that a character is three-dimensional and complex, that they have a story, and that they have a solid reason to exist in the story, other than mere tokenism.'

– Karl Iglesias, story consultant

So, you don't have to go far, especially online, to find people lamenting about the 'good old days', and the current conversation on diversity is no different. Even some writers think it's pointless or, as previously mentioned, 'political correctness gone mad', suggesting that publishing and production are solely about making money. In fact, they would not be wrong. The likes of Hollywood or the big publishers are not patrons of the arts; they actively want to make as much money as possible!

We've seen evidence of this again and again, with every 'hyped' book, movie or TV show. Some of these we will individually love; others we despise; others we will personally feel indifferent to. But when dealing with notions of audience, it's not about what we individually feel about a book, TV show or movie, but how the MOB feels about it. Sometimes, how the mob feels is almost counterintuitive, i.e. we buy it <u>because</u> we hate it! If this seems unlikely, just consider these four little words:

FIFTY SHADES OF GREY

It's pretty difficult to find anyone who admits to liking this book (though, believe it or not, they do exist: if you look on www. goodreads.com, you'll find *Fifty Shades* has an average 3.67 stars out of a possible five! This is from a whopping one and half MILLION ratings, with only 11% and 10% rated one or two stars, respectively). But some people dislike it so much they even have whole campaigns against it, such as *Fifty Shades of Abuse*, which says it 'normalises' manipulation, stalking, intimidation and even rape. Others think the story and/or writing is amusingly poor, creating parody Twitter accounts – *Fifty Sheds of Grey* is my personal favourite – as well as cartoons or memes that recut *that* (in)famous scene in the movie adaptation, when a suitably brooding Jamie Dornan tells a quivering Dakota Johnson, 'My desires are... unconventional.'

So, how come so many people bought the book? Now, I'm no psychologist, but I can hazard a good guess: plain old curiosity, not to mention what book reviewers call FOMO ('fear of missing out'). It's certainly why I bought it. Literally everyone was talking about it! How could anyone resist that? Now, I couldn't finish even the first of the trilogy, never mind the other two books – it remains at 45% on my Kindle to this day – though this is because of the standard of the prose, rather than any huge concerns about its sexual politics (and I agree, they are dodgy, even by my fairly libertarian, 'live and let live' standards!).

Now consider hype and diverse stories. Many of the most hyped stories in recent years, whether fiction, film or TV, have been diverse, especially when it comes to both female leads and race. The success of movies with strong female characters, like *Gravity* (2013) and *Lucy* (2014), have paved the way for more epic blockbusters like *Wonder Woman* and the *Black Widow* movie. We're also seeing more storyworlds that are populated almost entirely with BAME characters, such as *Empire* (2015) and *Luke Cage* (2016).

This is because diverse stories make money. The powers that be will make more of the same if they can get a return. It's that simple. So whether a writer feels diversity is important, or unimportant, it still adds up to the same thing: it's a very good idea to be as inclusive as possible in your writing, because more people will be interested. This potentially means more money... and studios, producers and publishers never say 'no' to that!

AUDIENCE 'DEAL BREAKERS'

'Ditch the tired old props. Grab the cup of tea from the old lady – and give her cocaine instead!'

– Mark Hill, author (@markhillwriter)

Authenticity is a key element of any characterisation, diverse or not. What audiences believe and will accept at any given time is all around us. The notion of the leery little old lady, like Mark Hill's quote, is perfectly acceptable nowadays. In British family movie *Paddington* (2014), comic favourite Julie Walters played this role as Mrs Bird, the Browns' housekeeper, who can weld as well as darn, not to mention drink grown men under the table. We laugh because it's unlikely, though at the same time all of us know very capable elderly women, so why not? Now imagine how Mrs Bird would have appeared 40 years ago... very differently, I'd wager, especially in a British film.

Other times, storytellers may want to go *against* the norms and values of the time, as in education and with outreach work. Obviously, this can sometimes work – especially when dealing with controversial issues. But ultimately novels, movies and TV shows tend to reflect the world around us; stories are about entertainment, first and foremost. This doesn't mean you can't use challenging themes and ideas in your work, but HOW you use them is paramount.

Grease (1978) might be a classic, but Sandy's transformation from good girl to wild child probably wouldn't be written that way today. I think we can ALL agree a modern audience finds the notion of 'changing for your man' (or, indeed, Danny attempting the same in reverse) rather icky and irrelevant some 40 years on. In contrast, consider a movie like *Legally Blonde* (2001). Despite being the best part of two decades old, this version of the protagonist who is a blonde girl in love has stayed remarkably fresh and relevant. This is because Elle is never once asked to change for the men in her life, even when it comes to her legal expertise. She is 'enough'. Thus, we can infer that the *Legally Blonde* version is what audiences expect and prefer.

Even in cases where characters do transform, it's worth putting HOW they transform under the microscope. In the case of an anti-hero like Gru from the *Despicable Me* franchise, it's true he is selfish and evil; but as we see, this is because his mother ignored and berated him as a child. Gru adopts the little girls Margo, Edith and Agnes for his own reasons (which are admittedly both selfish and evil), but of course is taught to be a better person through being a father figure to them. Crucially, however, when we consider Gru's transformation, we see it is only his selfishness and evil he is jettisoning; he is NOT changing personality. He is still eccentric, droll and a scientist, just the way the girls (and his minions) like him.

Audience acceptance of certain beliefs and values is key in getting them to accept certain stories and characters. As I've already mentioned, characters have to feel fresh AND relevant – if the character does not fulfil this last criteria, they will be disregarded. So, in the case of the 'Be Yourself' message, this is one of those 'deal breakers' I've mentioned. Modern audiences now, probably more than at any other time, believe a character changing directly for another character, like Sandy for Danny, is a BAD THING – no matter the story's context or genre.

IN A NUTSHELL: Challenging society's norms and values can be great BUT there are 'deal breakers', or certain things audiences simply won't compromise on. Find out what these things are in advance by examining consistently well-received published and produced content, which also sells well with audiences.

ALL-TIME FAVOURITES

'Whatever the race, colour, sexuality, disability – I don't care, as long as they are wonderful characters with a voice that sings.'

– Sam Copeland, literary agent (@stubbleagent)

So, while it's true, then, that we can only make generalisations and guesstimates when it comes to audiences, it's still worth thinking about WHO our work is for when thinking about diversity. Let's consider the top five highest-grossing movies of all time now. These movies have made more money than the average writer can comprehend – and that's just at the box office, with those sought-after cinema-ticket sales. At the time of writing, the top highest-grossing movies were:

1. *Avatar* (2009)
2. *Titanic* (1997)
3. *Star Wars: The Force Awakens* (2015)
4. *Jurassic World* (2015)
5. *Marvel's The Avengers* (2012)

According to *Box Office Mojo*, *Avatar* made $2,787,965,087 worldwide and *Marvel's The Avengers* $1,518,812,988 worldwide. Remember, we're not considering ancillary markets, such as DVD, streaming or merchandising (such as toys). This means the figure between the 'lowest' and highest figures is $1,269,152,099 – so *Avatar* made almost twice as much as *Marvel's The Avengers* at the box office. This is a truly jaw-dropping figure! But, as you are a writer, I would put money on your having watched *Avatar*. Everyone seemed to be talking about this movie back in 2009, plus mention it now and someone always has a wisecrack about 'Dances with Smurfs' or similar. But have you watched it? What about your work colleagues? Your parents? Grandparents? I ask because, even if they have all watched *Avatar*, <u>more people in the world have NOT watched it...</u> yet it is still the highest-grossing movie of all time.

Now, let's consider the top five books ever sold, in the same way. Obviously, books have been around for a lot longer than movies, so it's not really surprising that some of them are super-old. Check these out for size:

- *Don Quixote* (1605) by Miguel de Cervantes
  (500 million copies sold)
- *A Tale of Two Cities* (1859) by Charles Dickens
  (200 million copies sold)
- *The Lord of the Rings* (1954) by J.R.R. Tolkien
  (150 million copies sold)
- *The Little Prince* (1943) by Antoine de Saint-Exupéry
  (142 million copies sold)
- *Harry Potter and the Philosopher's Stone* (1997) by JK Rowling
  (107 million copies sold)

But even if we limit book sales to those written in 'modern times' – let's say the last 100 years – the top five still isn't wildly different. We end up with:

- *The Lord of the Rings* (1954) by J.R.R. Tolkien
  (150 million copies sold)
- *The Little Prince* (1943) by Antoine de Saint-Exupéry
  (142 million copies sold)
- *Harry Potter and the Philosopher's Stone* (1997) by JK Rowling
  (107 million copies sold)
- *And Then There Were None* (1939) by Agatha Christie
  (100 million copies sold)

- *The Hobbit* (1937) by J.R.R. Tolkien
  (100 million copies sold)

All of these books have been made into movies, TV series and short films, some multiple times. It's interesting that fantasy and action-adventure figures so highly on the list; I would have assumed crime fiction would have made more of a splash. I'm also surprised Charles Dickens's highest-selling title isn't *A Christmas Carol*, as that seems to be his most ubiquitous title (in my perception, anyway!). It really does prove you never can tell.

Anyway, how many have you read? I read a lot and can answer truthfully, just the one – you guessed it, the Agatha Christie. I do have a vague recollection of reading *The Little Prince* and *The Hobbit* at primary school, but I can't remember the plots of either, so I don't count them. I read half of *Harry Potter* to my son around the time it came out (before we abandoned it in favour of the *Captain Underpants* series, which was much more up our street). I also read approximately 50 pages of *The Lord of the Rings* around the time Peter Jackson's adaptations came out. The books are all great, I'm sure – I've met enough Potter fans and Tolkienites who insist they are, after all – but I'm just not interested in fantasy. Never have been!

So, even if your story is supposed to be for a mass audience, it's still not for 'everyone'. This is why publishers and producers deal in certain categories and styles, designed to hook various groups of people in to make that sale. Regardless of their efforts, there will still be people who will not be interested, just as there will be people who 'shouldn't' be interested, yet are. More on this, next.

ALL ABOUT THE £££$$$?

'What I'd love to see – and this is partly down to casting directors as well as writers and producers and directors – is for stories featuring diverse actors where the stories have nothing to do with diversity… Colour-blind casting and disability-blind casting. And writing.'

– Justin Young, TV producer and screenwriter

When writers say their stories are for 'everyone', they are making one of the most fundamental mistakes there is: that they can do whatever they want, in a crowded marketplace. Instead, scratch the surface and it will soon become obvious that these writers simply believe, erroneously, that their stories are somehow so innately interesting, people simply cannot resist their work. If this sounds arrogant or vain, it's because it is!

If we consider the top five highest-grossing movies again, we can see they're all much of a muchness in that they were heavily marketed at younger audiences. All of the main characters are in their teens to late twenties(ish). This is because young people have what marketers call 'disposable income' – i.e. they're more likely to have money to spend on stuff like cinema-going, rather than boring bills. So, if we discount *Titanic* as too icky and largely attracting young 'date night' couples, in the case of *Avatar*, *Marvel's The Avengers* and *Star Wars: The Force Awakens*, and (probably) *Jurassic World* (though it is considerably scarier than the previous three), a lot of parents will have been taking young children to see these films. Families mean at least one child with at least one parent, so that's potentially double the money. Parents have to accompany children under 12 to the cinema usually, so it makes a lot of economic sense to make family movies!

It's also no accident, either, that all five of the top-grossing movies are essentially action-adventures and special effects heavy. Younger audiences are much more demanding than previous generations in terms of general spectacle. Some children, as a result, are barely aware there was ever anything other than 3D animation; my boy, growing up in the noughties, asked when life 'became colour' – he thought the black and white images he saw on television were real! Poor CGI can kill off any potential franchise, plus kids are more media-literate than ever. They can decode images for meaning at much faster rates than today's adults can; plus they can spot gaping plot holes in just one viewing. My ten-year-old daughter was able to ask why Newt 'didn't just go to Arizona' with the 'dragon-bird-thing' in *Fantastic Beasts and Where to Find Them* (2016), instead of catching a boat to New York with his magic suitcase. 'Because then there would be no story' is the answer – but this is a rather poor answer when JK Rowling is setting the rules of her own storyworld!

Intriguingly, all five highest-grossing movies feature female leads prominently, with at least three female protagonists: Rose in *Titanic*, Rey in *Star Wars: The Force Awakens*, and Claire in *Jurassic World*. (Scarlett Johansson appears as Black Widow in *Marvel's The Avengers*, but she is the only female in the entire ensemble!) However, perhaps the most obvious thing about the top five highest-grossing movies is that they all feature white people in the main roles, with the obvious exception of *Star Wars: The Force Awakens*, which features black British actor John Boyega as Finn. This stretches to two if we consider Zoe Saldana, who is mixed race and plays Neytiri in *Avatar* (though, like Finn, she is not the protagonist, plus we never see her 'true' face).

So, if we're going to learn a lesson from Hollywood here, it's that if we want to attract the largest audience possible, it's all about the money. It would seem that, to get the most money and find a mass audience, stories 'need' to be:

- Action-adventures, thrillers and/or involving romance
- Epic in scope and feel
- Easily understood, with universal themes, i.e. 'good versus evil', 'love conquers all', 'you get what you deserve'
- Have relatable characters

Of course, you may not be interested in reaching a mass audience. You don't have to write stories you're not passionate about in order to make money. This would make you a hack. However, there's one thing from the list above that should interest EVERY writer – and that's the notion of 'relatability', especially if you want your story to feature diverse characters. I'll explain why, next.

KNOWING YOUR GENRE OR TYPE OF STORY

'Even the most boring identikit plot can be transformed by seeing it from a new POV, someone who experiences it differently.'

– Debbie Moon, TV screenwriter and showrunner (@DebbieBMoon)

There is a common belief, even within creative circles, that attracting an audience is simply blind luck. While luck does indeed play its part, with some creatives trusting to it more than others, there are still key elements that help writers find their audience, such as:

1) What types and groups of people would like your novel or screenplay?

There are loads of different genres and subgenres and markets now within fiction, film and TV. In turn, each of them has its own conventions and arouses certain expectations from its audience. Some will be entirely separate; others will have crossover elements. In addition, some will stand the test of time, while others will be more 'of the time' – a type of story an audience may want, but only for a limited period, going in and out of 'fashion', for want of a better word. So, if you write crime fiction, for example, you may find your novel, TV show or film being called a variety of different names, such as (but not limited to):

- **'Cosy'.** It might seem strange that stories involving the likes of murder might be called cosy, but this relates to the feel of the piece, especially the time period. Profanity will be mild and situations treated humorously, within small, close-knit-community storyworlds. The protagonist will nearly always be an amateur sleuth. Agatha Christie's *Miss Marple* series is cosy crime, as is Jessica Fletcher in TV's *Murder, She Wrote*.

- **Police procedurals.** This subgenre is usually realistic and set in the present day, with writers attempting to be as accurate as possible (while still using a certain dramatic licence) in representing crimes, including the aftermath and police procedures used in solving the case. Ian Rankin's *Rebus*, the novels and TV adaptation, is an example of the police procedural; we've also seen James Patterson's Alex Cross in several movie incarnations. First he was portrayed by Morgan Freeman in *Kiss the Girls* (1997) and *Along Came a Spider* (2001). Then he was replaced by Tyler Perry in the 2012 movie *Alex Cross*. Police procedurals may differ from the **military thriller**, which may take place in another location, like a courtroom, such as Aaron Sorkin's *A Few Good Men* (1992). Or it may not, such as in TV's *NCIS* franchise (2003–), which examines cases in a police-procedural manner, just within the military storyworld.

- **Hard-boiled.** In the hard-boiled subgenre of crime fiction, a detective works in a gritty, dark city and violence is explicit. Classic detective fiction such as that by Dashiell Hammett and Raymond Chandler comes under this category, but so do iconic movies like *Chinatown* (1972). Also crossing over with film noir, modern movies in this category include *The Usual Suspects* (1995), *Memento* (2000), *Drive* (2011) and *Nightcrawler* (2013). As far as television goes, it's often called 'neo noir' and favourites online include *Veronica Mars* (2004–7), *True Detective* and *Gotham*, which are both still ongoing at the time of writing. Foreign crime stories have also found new English-speaking audiences in recent years with the 'Scandi noir' or 'Nordic noir' phenomenon, exemplified by *The Killing*, *Borgen* and *The Bridge* on television, and the novels of such authors as Ragnar Jonasson, Stieg Larsson and Jo Nesbo.

- **Forensic thriller.** In this category, a pathologist or team will uncover various clues from the dead bodies he or she works with in order to help solve the case, which is usually a murder (though not always). In recent decades, these have been massively popular on TV, the *Crime Scene Investigation (CSI)* (2000–15) franchise being the most obvious. However, Patricia Cornwell's Kay Scarpetta novel series and the BBC's *Silent Witness* predate *CSI* by some margin, starting back in the nineties. The forensic thriller differs slightly from the **medical thriller**, which will usually centre around a hospital, without forensic elements. Authors such as Tess Gerritsen specialise in this subgenre of crime.

- **Domestic noir.** In this category, a (usually) female protagonist is up against a mystery of some kind, plus her lover or husband is probably implicated. This is a relatively 'new' subgenre, growing in popularity since the veritable explosion of interest in both *Before I Go to Sleep* (2011) by SJ Watson and *The Girl on the Train* (2015) by Paula Hawkins, both of which also became movies. These stories, whether books, movies or TV shows, are sometimes referred to as 'psychological thrillers'. This is because the protagonist in question will usually not be a policewoman, or detective, and nor is she an amateur sleuth. Instead she is pulled into the mystery against her will, usually as a direct result of the aftermath of a crime. My own novel, *The Other Twin* (Orenda Books), is domestic noir. Domestic noir on TV includes the recent *Doctor Foster* (2015) and *Apple Tree Yard* (2017).

<u>KEY TAKEAWAY:</u> Knowing exactly where your story falls within existing genres and the subgenres within them is absolutely crucial in finding your target audience. Knowing these genres and subgenres is also important: you cannot 'break new ground' if you do not know what has gone before! Equally, you must be well versed in the conventions and expectations of the genre you choose if you want your target audience to get onboard with you.

2) Identify other works LIKE your novel and screenplay – who are the main readers and/or viewers?

In the book world, publishers and agents may say 'It's all about the comps' – with 'comp' being short for 'comparisons' or 'comparables'. In other words, they want to know what previous book – preferably one that sold well and found its audience – yours is 'like'. It's a simple enough notion: if people liked that previous one, they should like yours, too. Producers of film and television may demand something similar from screenwriters, asking them in meetings for their 'reference' films or shows. It's obvious why: if you've ever spent even a fraction of time perusing adverts, or bookshelves and movie and TV Netflix and Amazon listings, you'll note phrases that are used again and again:

'Perfect for fans of [this BOOK/MOVIE/TV SHOW]'
'From the author of [that mega-bestselling BOOK]'
'If you liked [BOOK/MOVIE/TV SHOW], you'll love this!'
'From the producers of [that MOVIE or TV show you liked]'
'The next [*like* big bestselling BOOK/MOVIE/TV SHOW]'

Of course, just because a person liked one thing, does NOT mean they will automatically like another, even if the stories are similar. There are many different elements that separate two works, even if they're the same genre and type of story, or made/written by the same person. However, these elements are down to personal preference, rather than audience preference – so we're back to the notion of the individual versus the group, in effect.

People generally allow their individual preferences to take them into various audience groups. Why? Because there is simply too much content to choose from! I recall speaking to a friend who grew up in East Germany. When the Berlin Wall came down, he ventured into the west side of the city for the first time with his parents. They ended up going into a supermarket, where his mother promptly burst into tears while looking at the toothpaste aisle. When he asked his mother why she was crying, she answered, 'There's too much choice!' In East Germany, there had been perhaps two types of toothpaste, and that was it. Confronted with an abundance of choice for the first time in her life, my friend's mother felt lost and completely out of her depth.

It's the same when it comes to fiction, film and TV. Without categorising stories into genres and subgenres, we would literally not know where to start! So, consciously or not, we start to sort things according to how we personally like them, within the bigger groups of things available. That's why so many people claim ownership of their preferences within groups, too: sci-fi geeks; romance nuts; thriller junkies; horror fanatics and so on. Otherwise, we could spend our entire lives reading, or watching TV or movies, and not even manage to consume one per cent of it, especially considering it's being added to every single day. Handily for us writers, our potential audiences actively categorise themselves and their preferences – even if it's to say they have no specific preference and like an 'eclectic' mix (though, in real terms, it's nearly always LESS eclectic than they think!).

KEY TAKEAWAY: Knowing which prior works are comparable to our novel or screenplay means we can find out exactly what those audiences liked about those previous ones and utilise these things in our stories to their best advantage. Showing publishers, producers, agents and filmmakers we have this information demonstrates not only that we have our finger on the pulse of our target audience, but we know what we're talking about, too. What's not to like?

3) Can you drill down further from your main audience?

So, with reference to your own story, by now you know the genre (and, if applicable, subgenre and/or 'type' of story), plus comparable previous works. While we're dealing with a bunch of individuals when it comes to audience, this grouping of people allows us to make other assumptions and generalisations that may help in discovering what a 'typical' member of that audience may be like. This is where market research can come in handy.

The good news is, the internet was made for writers when it comes to questions like this! There's always market research being done and studies commissioned, so you can discover useful nuggets of information to get you started, simply by Googling. I discovered the following in less than five minutes:

- Mystery and crime is the most bought, most read type of fiction in the UK, though worldwide this is beaten by romance and/or erotica. Other popular genres that make a lot of money include horror and fantasy, especially as they are frequently part of series and sagas. Women are more likely to read mystery, crime, romance and erotica; whereas men are more likely to read horror and fantasy.

- In the UK, ebook sales fell for the first time in 2015 since the digital age began, and Waterstones declared it would stop selling Kindles in its stores. Despite doomsayers saying hardback and paperback books would become a thing of the past, this is apparently not true, with many readers still actively preferring them. Women are more likely to be Kindle users than men, intriguingly.

- Women make up 52% of cinemagoers in the USA and Europe. They generally stream more movies and television than men do, and women also watch more terrestrial TV in 'real time'; they also read more books than men. (This really begs the question of why some producers automatically think males aged 15–25 are the cash-cow generation!)

- Hispanic people go to the cinema the most, accounting for 25% of ALL US ticket sales, despite making up only 17% of America's population. It's not difficult to see why properties like the *Fast and Furious* franchise do so well with Vin Diesel at the helm and a large cast of Hispanic supporting characters. The so-called 'silver' or 'grey' pound of cinemagoers is not to be underestimated, either, with those in the 50–59 age group going most often.

- Children aged 2–11 are marketed at mercilessly when it comes to cinema (which I already knew) and, more surprisingly, apps! It seems toddlers and little kids know what they want and can twist Mummy and Daddy's arms to download it for them.

- Teenagers and young people under 25 watch most of their television and films on mobile devices, such as phones or tablets. If you have a teen in the house, you already know they never watch terrestrial TV and are likely to get all their news from social media, rather than radio.

- Though the stereotype is of the lone male video gamer, the gender split is actually roughly half and half! The percentage of men playing games is 50%, with the other half made up of 48% women (presumably the remaining 2% are gender non-confirming people, or perhaps aliens?)

Of course, these facts and figures are just the starting point for your own research. Some of these stats and studies will no doubt be familiar; you may have picked up on them being reported, even just within your peripheral vision. Others may seem common sense, because you're part of the community or group of people being studied. Others may seem far-fetched, or unlikely to you. This is where our own research, in real life, with real potential consumers, can really help. Again, this is where the internet can come in really handy (I don't know how writers and creators managed without it!).

KEY TAKEWAY: Checking which audiences are responding to which properties right now – and why – is key in deciding whom to target.

4) What's your USP? ('Unique Selling Point')

Another huge mistake writers make is rehashing stories that have already been told. This usually happens when they begin to understand the need for a target audience and comparables, and try to tell a story that's *like* another one, in order to get that elusive and important audience… but end up essentially retelling the story! Noooooo!

Publishers, producers, agents and filmmakers talk about 'the same… but different', but too many writers end up concentrating too much on the SAME and not enough on the DIFFERENT. As a result the stories feel stale, boring and derivative, even at concept level. Here are the same-old, same-old concepts I get pitched all the time:

1. **PITCH:** Wo/man with friend travels through time and space having various misadventures.

   MY RESPONSE: How is this different to *Doctor Who* or *Quantum Leap*?

2. **PITCH:** Loner detective character with a missing or dead spouse throws himself into solving cases because he can't save his loved ones.

   MY RESPONSE: How is this different from Peter James's Roy Grace *Dead* novel series, or TV's *The Mentalist*?

3. **PITCH:** Two detectives – one a sceptic, the other a believer – investigate weird goings-on to do with aliens or the supernatural.

   MY RESPONSE: How is this different to *The X Files* or *Aftermath*?

4. **PITCH:** In a society where women are subjugated by men and made into breeding machines, one woman takes a stand.

   MY RESPONSE: How is this different from *The Handmaid's Tale* by Margaret Atwood or *Only Ever Yours* by Louise O'Neill?

5. **PITCH:** A teenage girl discovers she has awesome powers of some kind and wrecks everything around her as someone comes after her.

   MY RESPONSE: How is this different to Stephen King's *Carrie* or Veronica Roth's *Divergent* trilogy?

6. **PITCH:** In a parallel or future universe, a group of evolved humans discover their powers and must decide to work WITH the human race, or AGAINST it.

   MY RESPONSE: How is this different to *The X-Men*, *Heroes* or *Misfits*?

It's important to note there is NOTHING WRONG with any of these concepts at grassroots level. They have created some really interesting and successful properties in fiction, film and TV, especially those that immediately come to mind in response. A person doesn't even have to be that familiar with the properties to know about them.

But if a writer wants to draw on any of these concepts, s/he absolutely has to find something NEW about it, or go home. Yet, too often, after pitching, the writer will eyeball me and insist theirs is somehow magically different... and I'll find out if I just read the script, or check out their book! A million times, NO. If you're a long-time reader of my blog, or have read my *Thriller Screenplays* book, you'll know what I'm about to say here: it's NOT the execution that counts when it comes to concept.

KEY TAKEAWAY: You have literal seconds to grab one of the movers and shakers with your concept. That's it. And if you don't? They will never get as far as even reading your submission. It's the same with your audience. So, if you're going to do 'the same... but different', you need that all-important USP, that *something* that sets your story apart from the rest and makes your target audience want to read it, or see it.

MARKET RESEARCH

'I'm fed up of seeing a wife/girlfriend being the killjoy who tries to talk the beefcake hero out of his "mission" and into staying home.'
– KT Parker, screenwriter and producer (@lunaperla)

Market research has always been part of the creative process. Discovering what audiences wanted – while never an exact science – was significantly harder to do in 'the olden days' of 15 or so years ago. It also took a lot more manpower, literally sending survey collectors out into the street, recruiting people for focus groups, test screenings and so on. This all still happens, but crucially takes a lot of time and money, so is usually out of the reach of the individual writer or smaller teams of creators.

The internet has changed all this. In the age of social media, there are unprecedented opportunities for individual writers to meet, converse with and hear the voices of their potential audiences.

Every day, millions of articles, blog posts, tweets, statuses, memes, pictures and more are posted about books, television shows, movies, web series, video games and other creative works. Where once writers and creators had too little input from potential audiences, they now arguably have too much – the new challenge is sorting 'the wheat from the chaff' as the old adage goes!

Now, the individual writer or small team of creators have access to market research tools through every step of the creative process, from planning through to publication or production. Writers can easily study their target audience via survey questions and polls online, or studies and reports. Writers can also send out research questions via email to fact-check with experts, or ask people about their lived experiences; they can follow marginalised groups' broadcasts via podcasts, YouTube channels, tweets and other online campaigns, even partaking in them where appropriate.

In short, the savvy writer has a huge number of tools at his/her fingertips to ensure they provide stories that seem relevant and authentic to their audience. While it's very easy to dismiss books, TV shows and movies that sell well, it's never because audiences are simply passive and suck up anything creators throw at them. If we look at all the failed books, TV programmes and movies – many of which had huge marketing behind them – we can see this is not the case. B2W reminds writers that finding an audience breaks down roughly into these three principles:

- It's not about 'selling out', but SELLING – that's what pro writers do
- It's always about the £££$$$. No one cares who the creator is or what the story is about if you can make that return
- If you have something 'worth' selling, people will buy it

When it comes to diversity, then, the current climate shows the average audience member is bored with the 'same-old, same-old'. They are actively looking for new, untold stories that feel fresh, relatable and authentic. But it is wise to remember, too, that storytelling is still entertainment, not education. Get up on your soapbox at your peril!

KEY TAKEAWAY: Market research is not about 'selling out', but rather finding what your potential audience is interested in, or bored with. What's not to like? But do remember that no amount of number-crunching or stats-pounding makes a good story, nor does getting up on your soapbox.

GETTING YOUR TARGET AUDIENCE TO COME TO YOU

'I think frequent gut checks will give a good indication if we're veering into stereotypes… Also "native speaker" checks – SO VITAL. Ask someone who lives that reality what they think of the character.'

– Sabina Giado, screenwriter (@SabinaGiado)

Crowdsourcing opinions and experiences via social media can create some wonderful interactions that feed your imagination. People are frequently very honest on both Twitter and Facebook, plus there are sites like Quora where people can talk in-depth about their lives. There are many people online who actively WANT to talk about their varied experiences and worldviews. Some activists will invite discussion; others will want to broadcast, so it's important to figure this out in advance; it's wise to listen first. Because there are so many trolls online, some people are justifiably wary of those from outside the community. Rather than crash into others' threads and ask specific questions in the first instance, it can be useful to maintain respectful parameters, following them initially and reading their threads, interacting with them generally first.

If time is of the essence for your project, or you have a very specific question, it can be useful to go to a figurehead or organisation within that community. This shows you have taken the time to look the community up and have those respectful parameters in mind. In the course of my research for this book, I went to organisations like @ Diversability, @diversevoices, @Writersofcolour, @EverydayAbleism, @WFTV_UK, @WomenWriters and @LGBTFdn, asking them to retweet to their followers. In the tweet, I simply wrote that I was writing about diverse characters and would love to hear people's experiences and/or favourite characters in novels, films and TV. This then meant people could get in touch with me if they wanted to share; I didn't pursue them with a barrage of questions.

KEY TAKEAWAY: Crowdsourcing REAL people's experiences, worldviews and thoughts can help your characters feel authentic and relevant, plus this is easier than ever thanks to social media. Just be respectful and mindful of the fact that making demands of people is not cool.

SURVEYS

'Any female who is only there as a "stakes" character for a male – trophy or victim – is offensive and dated. Also the religious fundamentalist hypocrite villain (secretly a paedophile or whatever) seems very tired.'

– **Lauri Donahue, script consultant and writer (@LauriDonahue)**

I find the quickest and easiest way to get my potential target audience's thoughts is to create a survey online and then invite interested parties to take it. There are countless sites where you can design your own survey, such as Survey Monkey, where you can make your survey questions as in-depth or broad as you like. I always allow people to tick the 'anonymous' box so they can speak candidly if they want to. (One caveat to all this is NEVER lift people's lives 'wholesale' into your work without permission. Either obtain that permission or mix several points of view or experiences together, to create a new one.)

Of course, some survey answers you collect will not be relevant or useful, but that in itself can tell you insightful things about your target audience. My crime novel *The Other Twin* originally started out as a YA novel about the online youth subculture based around depression and self-harm, which I was interested in at that time. I had designed a storyline based around a girl's blog, which I then focused my questions on. As I gathered approximately 200 responses over a three-month period, I discovered a common thread came up again and again: the people answering my survey were interested in solving crimes via the internet. My original storyline was not about a crime, but it got me thinking about a blog at the centre of a crime investigation, which is now the focus of my novel, which sold at auction with three publishers bidding for it. Clearly, those 200 responses were on to something! Most importantly, I didn't write the story BECAUSE those people wanted it, but because I loved the idea and wanted to write it as well.

KEY TAKEAWAY: Designing surveys can not only gain you helpful insights into your target audience, it can help shape your story. Giving people what they want is not 'selling out' if you want to write it.

YOUR IDEAL AUDIENCE MEMBER

'Pure angels and devils are dull, it's the spaces in-between that make for complex and compelling characters.'

> – Fritha Malcouronne, screenwriter (@NomadicWriter)

Before you can design a survey, or crowdsource opinions and thoughts (both in real life and on social media), you need to consider who your ideal audience member is in terms of a number of factors, such as age, gender, status, race and more. So, the next obvious step is to ask yourself who your story is more likely to appeal to, in terms of:

- **Age** – There's a big difference between children and teens, just as there's a difference between young people and older ones of 30+. Even more so when we get to 50+. This is all obvious stuff, with older and younger audiences having more money to spend generally.

- **Gender** – While it's true male and female tastes in film are not as far apart as they once were – women born in the eighties and nineties enjoy action and horror just as much as men now – there are still considerable differences in gender expectation, especially in novels and TV. That said, if women are consuming the most across the board, should we be placing more effort into appealing to *their* tastes? Or are we to assume they will watch and read our work regardless?

- **Ethnicity** – Just as women show up for female-centric pieces in film, it's been shown time and again that BAME audiences love movies marketed towards them. It's probably no accident, then, that shows with diverse casts on Netflix and Amazon also do well on this basis. Publishing in comparison is much more 'behind' on this, though there have been some recent steps to champion authors of colour and recruit more BAME talent, both in writing and within publishing.

- **Status, etc.** – Marriage, education, sexual orientation, disability, work status and more all may have an impact on the preferences of your ideal audience member. Obviously, the more specific your ideal audience member becomes, the more 'niche' your story will probably be.

KEY TAKEAWAY: Again, we can only deal in assumptions and generalisations when considering this ideal audience member, but s/he provides us with that all-important target to aim for when we're thinking of the best ways to both develop our story and sell it 'off the page' to publishers, agents, producers and filmmakers.

STORIES THROUGH THE AGES

'Writers should also be able to go back in history and accurately write for outdated viewpoints, true to the times, to the story.'
   – Graham Clegg, screenwriter and producer (@MrGrahamClegg)

Depending on what we're developing, as writers we know we can 'drill down' into our target audiences, using information gained from relevant market research, combining it with our comparables. But it's also important to realise that the way stories are told is also in constant flux. What might have seemed fresh and interesting as little as five years ago can now feel tired and stale to an audience. We must do our research to make sure we keep up to date with what is going on within the industry a) right now and b) in the past.

For example, if I were writing a horror movie that's a 'creature feature', I might be tempted to write a disparate group of characters, who are not friends, but are trapped in the lair with the monster for some reason, with a 'Final Girl' protagonist, like Ripley in *Alien*. Ripley was a huge surprise for 1979 and as a character has been enduringly popular with audience members, so an homage to her might seem like a no-brainer. But doing so might feel a little stale, because SO many movies have done this now over the last 35 years! Instead, I might do the exact opposite and have a Final Boy, as a surprise. Writer/director David Twohy did this in *Pitch Black*, with Riddick, even presenting the frame in such a way we don't realise it's Fry, our Ripley substitute, who is about to be carried away by the beast.

But then again, *Pitch Black* was almost 17 years ago (it's also more of a thriller than a horror), so now audiences are demanding something even more unusual. Consider, then, a modern horror movie like *It Follows* (2015), which introduces a female protagonist who is being hunted down by a sexually transmitted, supernatural force she doesn't understand, but which she knows she must never let catch her. She and her friends are trapped by the situation, rather than in a monster's lair, but, like their predecessors in *Alien* and *Pitch Black*, the friends have no choice but to vanquish the beast, just as in any good old-fashioned horror. Also, with reference to *Alien* (and less so to *Pitch Black*), *It Follows* is really interesting on a subtextual level, because horror audiences love 'layers' to their scares. Just as *Alien* asked us to consider the monstrous and life-threatening dangers within ourselves, such as cancerous tumours, *It Follows* asks questions about what it means to be a teen in today's sexualised culture, especially if you're female.

KEY TAKEAWAY: Though we're dealing with generalisations and assumptions about groups of people, that's the best we've got when it comes to the audience. To gain more perspective, then, 'drill down' into your main audience to discover a 'typical' audience member and what s/he might want from your story, via market research and your story's comps, but also by looking at which stories are feeling 'fresh' versus those that are feeling 'stale' right now.

SELLING, NOT SELLING OUT

'I wanted [my protagonist] to be normal. Someone I would share a glass of wine with. Who had flaws, but also an underlying strength.'

– Louise Jenson, author (@Fab_Fiction)

So, let's assume by now you have your own story and know the general ballpark group of people who will be interested in it. You hopefully have an idea of who your 'main' audience is via that ideal audience member: what he or she is like, plus what they have enjoyed before, plus what they are likely to enjoy in your story and why. You even known what your USP is and HOW your story is 'the same... but different' (with focus on the different!). This information is valuable not only in selling your idea 'off the page' to publishers, producers, agents and filmmakers, but in protecting your own vision and ensuring your story stays more or less the way *you* want it.

Every writer has a tale of disaster, in which their perfect story got ripped apart as it went to the market (sometimes, even before this). There is no cast-iron way to avoid this – we all know the English phrase 'too many cooks spoil the broth' – but there IS a way to make this LESS likely to happen to you. Yes, you've guessed it: by knowing your audience, what they want and why! Forewarned is forearmed – and if you know what your audience wants, you can compare and contrast this information with what you, as the writer, want.

Let's put this under the microscope in more detail. For the sake of argument, let's pretend you're writing a dystopian YA novel, in the vein of *The Hunger Games*, *Divergent* or *The Maze Runner*. Yours, like its predecessors, is highly visual with an 'epic' feel and sprawling storyworld; it has many potential opportunities, not only for movie or TV adaptations, but also to evolve into a franchise – let's start with a first novel, with a view to writing a trilogy.

Last, but by no means least, your cast is diverse, with a British East Asian teen boy of approximately 16 in the lead role, whom we'll name Chen, meaning 'great'. In the antagonist's role is the evil Baroness, a white, grown woman who is ageless, not unlike the White Witch from C.S. Lewis's *The Lion, the Witch and the Wardrobe*, who scared the bejesus out of you as a kid. In terms of main secondary characters, Chen has two female friends who help him, whereas the Baroness has two evil henchmen on her side.

Remember, knowing what's gone before and how audiences responded to it will help you sell your own idea 'off the page'. For example, dystopian YA usually features a female protagonist like Katniss Everdeen from *The Hunger Games*, who is now so iconic it's no surprise the vast majority of works in this subgenre also feature female leads. Remember – if the industry finds something works and audiences want it, they will keep on doing it. This is why we have the likes of Tris in the *Divergent* trilogy, Cassia in the *Matched* trilogy, and Sephy in the *Noughts and Crosses* series.

In comparison, *The Maze Runner*, both the book and resulting movie adaptation, is notable for going against the grain by having not only a male lead, but a (mainly) all-male cast. This is unusual for YA, dystopian or not. On the other hand, it could be argued that *The Maze Runner* has more in common with classic 'speculative fiction' like *Lord of the Flies* by William Golding than *The Hunger Games* or *Divergent*. 'Spec fic' is a broad category of narrative fiction that includes elements, settings and characters created out of imagination and speculation rather than based on reality and everyday life. (I've always thought this a bizarre category, because since when has fiction not been created out of 'imagination and speculation'? I suspect 'spec fic' is what they called 'dystopian' before that tag was broadly used by the publishing industry, followed by film and TV makers.) Whatever you want to call it, though, the link is clear: we have a disparate bunch of boys, marooned in a place they don't want to be, ergo *The Maze Runner* is '*Lord of the Flies*... in a maze'. The same... but different, remember!

You decide to submit your novel as a cross between *The Maze Runner* and *Divergent*, with a side order of *Harry Potter*. Chen is The Chosen One, in effect: only he can save the world from the evil Baroness, who is intent on draining him of his magical powers in order to power her machine, which will make mindless drones/zombies of the entire population.

WHAT THEY WANT VERSUS WHAT YOU WANT

'It's okay to talk about things that are different, the problem is assigning a moral judgement.'

– Alex Clare, author (@_AlexandraClare)

So, you've submitted your novel and agents are queuing up to talk to you about it. They love your concept and think the dystopian storyworld is really cool. They think it's commercial and will sell well. They also think there is room for movie adaptations or TV show tie-ins. All is looking great. But now you need to choose the agent you believe will do his or her best for the story in the marketplace, so, to help you decide, you have to sift through the feedback you've got. Most of it, as you might expect, centres around Chen, your protagonist, and the Baroness, your antagonist. The questions are as follows:

1. Could Chen be female?

This is not an unreasonable request. As we've already established, most YA dystopian novels have a female lead. If you're not especially attached to Chen's gender, it probably would be a good idea to switch him from male to female. After all, your target audience is predominantly female teen girls – and the numbers say, exceptions like *The Maze Runner* aside, that teen girls like teen girl leads in their dystopian YA.

<u>**VERDICT:**</u> (Probably) yes.

2. Could Chen be white?

Now we're on dodgier ground. While most female leads in YA are white, is there a genuine reason for this? Do more white teen girls buy dystopian YA? It's hard to tell, especially when there is so little choice available, with so few diverse leads in dystopian YA – or indeed any genre – and with white women so frequently standing for 'all women'. If Chen were to remain male and be white, the issue is either better or worse, depending on your standpoint: better, because, even though he's white, there are far fewer white male leads in YA; or worse, because there are waaaaaay more white male leads across all stories.

<u>**VERDICT:**</u> Nope. Back the hell up!

3. Could we change Chen's name?

Now, Chen is an obviously East Asian name, which can act as a handy marker for his ethnicity in the story. But just as many people of colour living in English-speaking countries won't have names like this, because they're European or American, having been born there. Plus, as any EFL teacher will tell you, even Chinese people will choose their own alternative English names. So, it would *not* be inauthentic to change Chen's name to something more American or European. Names like Edward, Darren or Rory also mean 'great' (or a version of this). A more European or American name might also 'connect' more with your target audience, even if they have East Asian heritage themselves.

<u>**VERDICT:**</u> Yes.

4. Could the Baroness be a man instead?

Online feminist critique sometimes suggests female characters have to be 'role models' and 'positive'. This leads to some commentators suggesting it's misogyny to cast women in the antagonist's role (an accusation levied at Gillian Flynn for *Gone Girl*). But it is not an act of malice to cast anyone in the antagonist's role; it is just a character role function. Also, remember you modelled the Baroness on your childhood fear, the White Witch. To change her to male would be the ultimate betrayal of your original vision – your very own 'deal breaker'.

VERDICT: Not a chance!!!

5. Does the Baroness HAVE to have lost a child?

Writers can utilise well-known tropes and motifs to their advantage, especially as 'short cuts' in whole new storyworlds, like dystopia, fantasy and science fiction. In addition, audiences are frequently asked to forgive antagonists for their behaviour, especially if they're female – in the case of witches and magical queens and other types of supernatural women, they are frequently grieving mothers (presumably because of fairy tales). This will be why they hate the world and want to burn it down. So this trope feels stale and perhaps it would be more refreshing if the Baroness were a megalomaniac, like her classic male counterparts?

VERDICT: Let's change it.

6. Could Chen's two friends compete for his (romantic) attentions?

A love triangle frequently figures in YA generally, so this note makes sense. Two girls competing for his attention, however, sounds a bit stale, plus there will always be a loser. This could leave a nasty taste in the mouths of our target audience, as they may still believe in happy endings. However, if Chen were gay and neither girl was ever in with a chance, this could create something not often seen in YA – plus we could avoid any icky sexual frisson between the evil Baroness and Chen in their confrontations.

VERDICT: Why not (but let's twist it).

Obviously, there could be any number of feedback points, but these are the ones that catch your eye as being the most relevant, especially when it comes to diverse characters. Your own verdicts here will help you pick the agent you feel 'gets' your story the most. A lot of it will be gut feeling and that's okay. If you pick the one you believe will fight for your story the best when it goes out to market, to publishers (and beyond), the more likely things will end up the way you want. That's not to say it will end up 'perfect' – there may be other decisions down the road you don't like – but sticking with your gut instincts and imposing 'deal breakers' (like point 4, above) is one example of selling, not selling out.

A NOTE ON LUCK

'For me, a good character is flawed and believable.'

– Matt Wesolowski, author (@ConcreteKraken)

The likes of Hollywood and the big publishers are risk averse because they never trust solely to luck. This doesn't mean they never misfire; they have a great many failures – probably more numerous than their big hits, in fact. But those big hits will bring their failures out of the dirt, with some properties even making up their losses as time goes on.

The biggest names in fiction, film and TV find their target audiences and relentlessly pursue them, first via the actual writing of the products they will go on to market. This is a lesson ALL writers can learn from big-name publishing and production. What I have outlined so far on audiences and doing your research is not rocket science. These things are simple and straightforward, but boring to many writers, which is why they don't do them. So it stands to reason that, if you do, you will be one step ahead of most writers, not only in writing diverse characters (and hopefully keeping them that way), but in getting your story published or produced. As Hollywood A-list actor Denzel Washington says, 'Luck is when an opportunity comes along and you're prepared for it.'

EXCUSES, EXCUSES

'Good representation and diversity is really about creating VARIETY... Diversity within the diversity!'

– Vinay Patel, screenwriter (@VinayPatel)

Every time someone mentions target audiences, writers come out of the woodwork on forums, message boards and social media with various objections, such as:

- I don't want to write FOR the marketplace
- Being commercial means selling out
- My story is arthouse (even though it's not)

The above are just excuses from writers who don't want to have to do the work at foundation level. It's true that hacks exist, writing without care, but considering the target audience doesn't make you one. You can find your target audience and give them what they want, without EVER selling your creative soul. So, to recap, consider:

- What is your story's logline? What other stories are like yours and why? How is yours 'the same... but different'?

- What other characters, themes, messages are like yours? Why?

- How well did these previous works do? When was this? What has changed since (if anything) socially? Culturally? Is the story beginning to feel stale? How can you twist it and make it seem fresh?

- Who are the types of people that would like your story? Why? Are there any 'deal breakers' for your audience – i.e. age, gender, status, etc. of the characters? Or the type of story, or the way it's told?

- Why do YOU want to tell this story? What is important or authentic about it? What is entertaining about it?

There's another phrase, 'the harder I work, the luckier I get', which some people believe originated with big-shot Hollywood producer Samuel Goldwyn. He is also reported to have said 'Let's have some new clichés'. So, rather than cross your fingers and hope for the best, don't trust in luck, either – and you'll be more likely to be on hand to deliver those stories that will eventually get called stale and clichéd!

SUMMING UP

✓ Diverse characterisation doesn't have to mean stories solely about 'issues'. Instead, it's about reflecting the variety of people and their worldviews in our diverse world.

✓ Audiences' perception of characterisation is changing: they no longer necessarily want white, straight males at the heart of EVERY story in fiction, film or TV.

✓ Character diversity does not necessarily *have* to feed directly into the story's plot, but can form part of the storyworld or even be incidental.

✓ If drama is conflict – and it is – this does not mean your story or characters have to be 'positive' or 'role models'. Besides, there will be multiple interpretations of your characters and story anyway by the time it gets to publication or production.

✓ The most hyped stories aren't always the best stories. Don't worry about the stuff you like or dislike, if you haven't written it. Focus instead on how those pieces found their audiences and what lessons you can learn from them.

✓ Diverse stories make money. The industry is not a patron of the arts, or an educator for change. Instead, what audiences want, they tend to get, as they vote with their wallets, directly or indirectly.

✓ Stories that are intentionally inclusive, rather than political, often create the most authentic, relevant characterisation, which target audiences respond to. 'Relatability' is critical, on a literal or metaphorical level, in the best characterisation.

✓ Writers need to understand what has gone before, to avoid 'rehashing' old stories, tropes and characters. We need to stay up to date with what audiences have liked, but also deliver twists on their expectations. This is only possible by immersing ourselves in our genres, subgenres and favourites.

✓ Our works need their own unique selling points – publishers and producers might want 'the same... but different' but there are too few scripts in the pile that are DIFFERENT enough.

✓ Research and crowdsourcing people's opinions, worldviews and experiences is easy in the social media age. Just be beware of co-opting those opinions, worldviews and experiences as your own. Use them as a springboard instead.

✓ Understanding target audiences and how they work doesn't make you a hack, nor does it mean you're 'selling out'. Always write about what you're passionate about; just bear in mind who you are writing for as well.

✓ Pinpoint in advance what your own 'deal breakers' are when it comes to your diverse characters and the story they are in. This will help you see who has the same vision as you in getting your work to its audience – publishers, agents, producers and filmmakers. Preparation always pays off!

HEROES, SHEROES AND VILE VILLAINS:
THE PROTAGONIST AND ANTAGONIST

'We don't see things as they are; we see them as we are.'

– Anais Nin

MAIN CHARACTERS AND DIVERSITY

Historically, main characters are the *least* diverse in most stories, especially film, but even novels and TV, too. Generally speaking, protagonists and antagonists (both originating in and destined for audiences in the Western, English-speaking world) will be:

- Male
- White
- Straight
- Able-bodied

It's easy to see how the above intersects with the 'top four' in the current discussion on diversity. There are, of course, notable exceptions:

- **Race.** In novels, white women tend to take the helm if there is a female lead. In movies, BAME characters may take the spotlight as protagonist, but usually more often if they are men and of African descent. Actors such as Denzel Washington, Will Smith and Chiwetel Ejiofor tend to occupy a multitude of roles, both heroic and 'worthy', taking in action-adventure, thriller, comedy and drama, especially biopic and/or true story. In TV, some female BAME characters can be found, though they are more often in US TV shows and part of an ensemble cast. Women of colour are typically protagonists such as Olivia Pope in *Scandal* (2012) or Cookie Lyon in *Empire* (2015); or animated, such as Dottie in *Doc MacStuffins* (2012). It's unusual to find female BAME characters who are also antagonists, like Mariah in 2016's *Luke Cage* (known as 'Black Mariah' in the comics).

- **Gender.** There is more gender parity of female characters in television than film, especially when it comes to soap opera and other precinct drama. Though female authors generally lack the awards or critical acclaim awarded to male authors (particularly those writing literary fiction), there are now many more female protagonists and antagonists than there were even ten years ago, not just in romance or so-called 'chick lit', but also crime fiction, mystery/thriller and horror.

- **LGBT.** If lesbian, gay or transgender characters take the spotlight as protagonists in TV or movies, it's most often as part of a 'coming-out' or transition story. In the past, LGBT characters were sometimes antagonists, but this trend seems to have fallen off in recent years. The most recent I can think of is Brendan in *Hollyoaks* (2010–13), a gay anti-hero whose violence and underhand dealings were nothing to do with his sexuality, but the vicious gangster underworld he lived and operated in. In novels, a whole subgenre of 'queer YA' has emerged, aimed at teens and with LGBT characters in lead roles, though, again, many focus on coming-out and transition. There seem to be very few stories across all mediums and genres where a protagonist or antagonist's homosexuality is incidental.

- **Disability.** Again, if a protagonist has a disability, this most often has a direct impact on the story, across all mediums, especially with reference to drama and struggle. Disabled protagonists will often take their lead from true story and real life, such as the recent biopic of Stephen Hawking, *The Theory of Everything* (2014). Occasionally, genre heroes have incidental disabilities that form plot points in the narrative, especially (interestingly) if they have a bionic arm, such as Furiosa in *Mad Max: Fury Road* (2015), Spooner in *I, Robot* (2004) or Bucky in the *Captain America* franchise. TV characters also sometimes have incidental disabilities, such as the lead in *House* (2004–12). In novels, disabled main characters are most often men and wheelchair users, from Sir Clifford in *Lady Chatterley's Lover* (1928) through to Will Traynor in the novel and film *Me Before You* (though neither is the protagonist). Disabled antagonists are generally at a premium nowadays, unless we count mental health – then they're everywhere, in all mediums! They're usually violent 'Others', especially serial killers in the tradition of Michael Myers from *Halloween* (1978), whether they wear actual masks or not.

IN A NUTSHELL: Protagonists and antagonists don't tend to be diverse, so making a small switch can make all the difference. Remember, though, that focusing *too much* on the diverse nature of your character is just as wearying as focusing on it too little!

BAD GIRLS

With female leads, there is frequently an onus on them to be 'better' than male leads (even within the same type of story), because of that pesky belief they should be 'positive' and 'role models'. YA author Julie Mayhew (@juliemayhew) spoke with me about this and posited, 'I would like to see more "problematic" female characters. Let's have characters feeling what they feel, right or wrong. I read too many female characters who are just the vessel for an issue or a message.' I'm with Julie. It seems like reviewers of novels, movies and TV shows in particular can be particularly harsh on female leads who are morally ambiguous, selfish or screwed up, saying they're 'unlikeable' and that they 'didn't care' about them... yet, frustratingly, male leads with EXACTLY the same characteristics can be celebrated, as if their male-ness gives them a 'get out of jail free' card.

So, it's definitely more difficult to get a badly behaved female lead greenlit than a goody two-shoes, it's true. But enough writers have declared war on the 'positive' female lead to make it worth creators' time to swim against the tide. Despite internet critiques demanding that women be 'good', there is a rich literary tradition of renowned anti-heroines every schoolkid will know, from Shakespeare's Lady Macbeth through to Charlotte Bronte's Jane Eyre. This means it's not difficult to see why literature today has a small but significant contingent of bad girls who may be unreliable narrators, morally ambiguous, enigmatic, difficult and/or completely untrustworthy.

Pushback against the 'good girl' trope has always been there, but has seemed to rocket forward in the last five to ten years with such iconic female leads as Lisbeth Salander from Stieg Larsson's Millennium trilogy. Intriguingly, most of these literary bad girls will find themselves remade in movie and TV adaptations of their stories, which is another point in favour of writing a much more diverse female character.

To sum up, if you find yourself wanting to challenge the status quo, ask yourself if you are the only one to do so. Chances are you won't be, so there are lessons you can learn from writers who have been there before you. This will also give you confidence and enable you to make informed decisions about what is – and isn't – important to you as you struggle to get your diverse character 'off the page' and to your prospective target audience. I did this with my own bad girl protagonist, Poppy, in my novel *The Other Twin*. When feedback came in, saying the publishers 'could not identify' with her, I knew I just needed to stay calm. I had done my research and spent a long time designing and writing Poppy as a character. In real terms, there's nothing THAT unusual about Poppy: she can be selfish and reckless, but also loyal and fierce. I know women like her and I knew the right publisher would identify with her. This, of course, happened and *The Other Twin* sold to Orenda Books at auction in August 2016 – so, from no one wanting it, eventually three publishers did!

IN A NUTSHELL: It's a sad fact that female leads are often held to a higher standard and subjected to more scrutiny than male characters (even by those who call themselves feminists and/or progressive!). Make sure you do your research on this to make an informed decision – then forget about the naysayers.

CHARACTER MOTIVATION AND BACKSTORY

Every protagonist needs a goal, want or desire of some kind, for some reason; plus, every antagonist needs to counter that goal, want or desire, too. This is characterisation 101, the very basics. (Obviously, there will be certain differences according to such things as the medium you're working in, or the genre or type of story or characters you're writing.) In comparison, backstory is a history or background for that character. Backstory most often refers to events BEFORE the story that may help inform or even directly affect events IN the story playing out in front of the reader or audience via the book, movie or TV programme.

When it comes to the protagonist and antagonist of any story, in whatever medium, there are certain motivations and backstories for main characters that crop up again and again. The following have got very stale and need a shake-up in my view:

- **Swarthy hero with a dead wife or girlfriend (or family).** Dead loved ones have become a shorthand for hero angst and desire to make the world pay. That's not to say you can't use this idea, but, if you do, make sure it's not the same-old, same-old. Do your research!

- **Vulnerable heroine who's been sexually abused/raped.** Sexual violence as a motivating factor for female leads has been done to death, plus potential audiences on social media are making it clear they feel this trope has had its day. Use at your peril in the current climate.

- **[Negative-adjective] female lead with tragic backstory.** Female leads with dead (female) children and sisters dominate the spec pile, just as they do in produced content. Instead of being super-angry like their male counterparts, they may be 'guilt-ridden' and/or 'depressed' – the aforementioned 'negative adjective'. Interestingly, they hardly ever have dead sons, brothers, husbands or boyfriends. A tiny change there could make all the difference.

- **Insane villain with a screwed-up plan.** Villains are too often simply insane, trying to take down the protagonist and/or the world for reasons known only to themselves. While insanity can work as a motivating factor for your villain, there needs to be some kind of logic to his/her plan, so potential readers and audiences can follow it. Also, villains don't wake up thinking, 'Aha! I am evil'... They think they're the good guy – and our hero is the baddie. Can you reflect that in your antagonist? If you can, you're in the minority in the spec pile.

IN A NUTSHELL: Just four motivating factors and backstories dominate fiction, film and TV when it comes to heroes and villains. Try banning yourself from using these, or flip it – see where this takes you instead.

CHARACTER ROLE FUNCTION

So, when it comes to characterisation generally, writers usually have some instinctive idea of how role functions work, especially when it comes to the protagonist and antagonist. The notion of 'good versus evil' or 'goodies versus baddies' is universal, no matter our backgrounds, whether cultural, religious, educational, or financial. As starting points go, it's obvious. From these 'major' characters, writers then (again, obviously) need a supporting cast of minor characters. How we describe this may be varied, but the three ways I see discussed most often are:

- Major, minor, peripheral
- Primary, secondary, tertiary
- Main, supporting (major/minor)

Or sometimes a combo of the above. On my site at www.bang2write. com, I most frequently talk about main characters, secondary characters and peripheral characters – but it really doesn't matter what you call them, just that you know who is who, who does what, and why.

'TYPICAL' DIVERSE CHARACTERS AND PLOTS

When it comes to the top four diverse characters and the plots that involve them, there are 'go-to' stories that appear in the spec pile and in published and produced content, over and over again:

- **Race.** With black characters who are African-American, we may have 'feelgood' movies about sport (usually basketball), but most often stories in the spec pile concern slavery, prison or gangs. If set in the UK, stories involving black characters will often present them as poor. With Asian characters, the two plots – or situations – of choice are usually honour killings and/or arranged marriage... I see very few screenplays involving characters who are Hindu, though I have seen quite a few unpublished novels. I hardly ever see stories involving East Asian characters from places like China or Japan, though when I do it's as kick-ass martial artists, and/or Triad or Yakuza gang members in thrillers. Otherwise, most stories involving BAME characters will be drama, rather than genre, and highly realistic.

- **Gender.** Of the 'top four' diverse character types, female characterisation has possibly made the best inroads in recent years... IF you consider white women as standing for 'all women'. Though there have been many varied representations of women – gone are the days, it seems, of 'women's stories' – frustratingly, nearly all the most well-known, celebrated, money-spinning female leads have been white. It's time to intersect gender with race to bring more varied and interesting leads across all mediums.

- **LGBT.** Stories with LGBT characters will again usually focus on realism and drama. Gay men will feature in some comedies, especially rom-coms, in the mentor role. Coming-out stories heavily feature gay protagonists, as do stories of transition when characters are transgender. Stories of trans women wildly outnumber those about trans men, plus trans women are often sex workers. There are very few stories about young trans people or children. Stories about non-binary and gender queer people – those who do not identify as male OR female – are largely non-existent as far as I can see in the spec pile AND published and produced content.

- **Disability.** Sometimes dubbed 'inspiration porn' by disability activists, disabled characters most often appear in drama stories as wheelchair users and those with learning disabilities. The protagonist will be a Change Agent – think *Forrest Gump* – and teach those around him (and it's nearly always a him). Will Traynor in the book and subsequent movie adaptation of *Me Before You* by Jojo Moyes is another classic example. Women with disabilities don't tend to get much of a look-in in this subcategory, though they do appear in soap operas in more 'ordinary' roles – mums, sisters, friends (though rarely leads). Actors who are also little people, like Warwick Davis and Peter Dinklage, have done a lot to cement disability as part of the storyworld in the fantasy genre; the character of Dr Trask – previously cast as a man of normal height – was recast without comment with Dinklage in *X-Men: Days of Future Past* (2014). Generally speaking, though, to be disabled in the average storyworld is to be doomed and/or dissatisfied.

No doubt you will recognise these typical plots and characters from published and produced content yourself. Again, there have been some GREAT stories with these characters – the issue is not that they exist at all, just that there are TOO MANY examples of the same-old, same-old.

IN A NUTSHELL: Audiences have started to demand more VARIETY, so an obvious thing to do to make your own diverse characters stand out is avoid these 'classic' plots where they appear.

PERIOD PIECES AND HISTORICAL FICTION

Many writers, filmmakers and creators believe – erroneously – that they cannot be as diverse as they would like to be when it comes to period pieces. They may think that people of the past were much more homogenous than they are now, when in reality nothing could be further from the truth. Historian Greg Jenner, author and chief advisor to the BBC's *Horrible Histories* programme, points out: 'If you write a story set in the past, there's a decent chance at least one of your characters could be a person of colour, or perhaps an immigrant, or both. It's not political correctness to increase casting diversity, it's actually a matter of historical accuracy.'

So, diversity has ALWAYS been part of human life! The only difference is that only one voice – that of white people, especially men – has dominated Western storytelling. Consider these points:

- **Race.** Though there are no periods in British shared national history when whiteness wasn't the dominant ethnicity, the story of Britain is the story of immigration, going all the way back to the Ice Age. There were black people here in Tudor times, such as Henry VIII's trumpeter. By the eighteenth century, there were thought to be around anywhere between 4,000 and 50,000 black people living in Britain, many of whom came here as servants and slaves to wealthy masters. According to Jenner, it was even thought very fashionable to have a black footman wear your livery when serving dinner guests! There was also a large influx of South Asian people, following the British Empire's involvement in India; plus the expertise of Chinese sailors in the tea industry, which also saw many East Asian immigrants settling in London from the late 1700s onwards. This gave rise to the emergence of Chinatown in London as far back as the 1880s. There were also frontiersmen in the American Wild West who were black, alongside more famous icons like Hugh Glass (he's the guy who got savaged by the bear in *The Revenant*, 2015). So, really, there's absolutely no excuse for an endless sea of white faces, just because you're writing a period piece!

- **Gender.** Women have done surprising things they're not 'supposed to' throughout history, with multiple myths created about them, too. Consider the Amazon warriors, the basis for DC Comics' *Wonder Woman*; not to mention Joan of Arc or Boudicca – and that's just for starters. There are many women in history whose amazing untold stories are just waiting to be uncovered, either via biography and biopic, or as inspiration for your own female characters.

- **LGBT.** Gay men and women have always been persecuted for their sexuality, so some writers and creators believe they must have hidden this aspect of themselves from the world to avoid detection. Nothing could be further from the truth. The Victorians had what were known as 'molly houses' – meeting houses for homosexual men. There have been many famous gay women, too, such as Frida Kahlo, Patricia Highsmith and Virginia Woolf. Some people also believe transgender people are 'new' – again, this is not true. There have always been transgender people! The Native Americans called it 'two spirits' and it was considered a great honour.

- **Disability.** In current period pieces, the average character seems to adhere to the notion of 'survival of the fittest'. If disabled characters appear at all, they nearly always die due to poor nutrition and/or healthcare. But again, this is not accurate. There were many people in the past who survived terrible accidents and horrifying conditions and diseases, who would be termed 'disabled' today. The great military commander Hannibal, of the ancient city of Carthage, had only one eye (some sources say he cut it out himself!); Admiral Nelson had only one arm after his elbow was shattered in battle; plus the aforementioned Hugh Glass undoubtedly had at least a lasting limp from his bear mauling. Franklin D. Roosevelt survived polio and used a cane; poet Lord Byron had a club foot, making walking extremely difficult; and Thomas Edison was thought to have a learning disability, but this didn't stop him inventing countless things we use today, such as the light bulb.

But don't take my word for it – check out your local library, museums and the internet for inspiration! Samantha Horley (@ SamanthaHorley), a writer, script consultant and former sales agent with SALT and Summit Entertainment, agrees:

> I was hired to give feedback on a female-centric period piece set mid-last century based on real events... however, their wish list cast was ALL white and posh. I did some Googling and quickly found there were black Brits at the time, mostly first-generation West Indians... there was literally no reason for this period piece not to be diverse. These could be characters, people, who were there and significant, not token. Before, the project had felt very dated, creatively. Now it feels not just contemporary, but more commercial. It's a film I'd want to see because it's a story I've not seen before. And that's the key.

IN A NUTSHELL: There are diverse, untold stories all throughout history, ripe for the picking to inspire you. Discount nothing.

STEREOTYPES

Working with writers, I've discovered over the years that many worry about stereotyping characters – especially diverse characters – in their work. This is not surprising, especially in the social media age when this word is used with abandon by critics and audience members alike. It would seem, at first glance, that *every* popular character is derided with such words at some point, so writers shouldn't bother worrying about it. But this is complacency, pure and simple. As with working out our target audiences, we need to do our foundation work and due diligence when it comes to all aspects of what characterisation means, if we are to avoid those classic pitfalls.

As you no doubt know, stereotypes are widely held, but fixed and oversimplified, images or ideas of a particular type of person, or thing. Check out the language used there: 'fixed' and 'oversimplified'. Obviously, no one wants THAT in their characterisation! Characters need to feel authentic and vital, diverse or not. However, you may be using stereotypes in your writing of diverse characters if you have:

- Characters from ethnic minorities speaking in pidgin English and/or performing servile roles to white people. In contrast, they may be in charge instead – hence the plethora of black police chiefs, dating back to the eighties at least

- Female characters who revolve solely around the men or children in their lives

- LGBT characters as highly sexually promiscuous loners, who are deeply unhappy

- Disabled characters who are incredibly bitter and die by suicide (especially wheelchair users)

Note that simply filling these roles does not mean automatically the character is a stereotype. The above is not to say you can NEVER use these tropes. There have been some well-rounded, three-dimensional diverse characters who have *begun* exactly at these points. But that is the key: it's a starting point, not the whole character.

Also, when it comes to diversity, it would be nice to see characters OUTSIDE these parameters once in a while. Why do we always see BAME people at either end of the scale – servants or in charge? Why not a female lead whose partner or husband supports her ambitions? Why not LGBT characters who have monogamous relationships? Why not a disabled character who is not suicidal? What could your story gain from these small changes?

IN A NUTSHELL: Avoid stereotypes altogether by ensuring your diverse characters don't begin in the 'same-old' places in the narrative. Identify which are the most used when thinking about a specific diverse character, then mix it up to make it feel 'fresh'.

STOCK CHARACTERS

'Stock character' and 'stereotype' are frequently used interchangeably, especially on the internet in reviews and critiques. This is because a stock character is a stereotypical person whom audiences readily recognise from frequent recurrences in particular genres, subgenres and types of story. Stock characters are conventional and underdeveloped because the writer is relying on the audience's existing knowledge when it comes to interpreting who they are (and how they will probably act in the story, plus why). Examples of stock characters may include: boy/girl next door; child prodigy; fall guy; town drunk; mad scientist; jock; tart; bad boy; battle-axe; Tiger Mom; shrew; wise tramp and so on. If you have used these words yourself, this is because in real life we attach labels to people, for various reasons, some good, some bad, some neutral – so you can kind of understand why writers might use them, too, as a kind of 'shortcut' to characterisation.

All this being said, knowing your stock characters has an unexpected bonus, especially when you're considering how to 'twist' your target audience's expectations. Using them as a starting point can be really effective IF you put them in a genre or type of story where we don't expect to see them. Joss Whedon is a master of doing this. Even in a car crash of a movie like *Alien Resurrection* (1997), we can still see his unusual characterisation expertise at work. Whedon's band of 'space pirates' is as diverse and progressive as previous instalments in the franchise. Ripley's 'Final Girl' status was cemented in movie history and Parker, the *Nostromo*'s sole African-American, was unusual in 1979 for NOT dying first, so Whedon draws on both of these things, adding feminism and potential homosexuality to the mix, two things we definitely did not expect back in the nineties. With android Call's talk of 'burning her modem' we're reminded of Germaine Greer's call to arms to feminists to burn their bras; plus Vriess and Christie's bromance is on show before the word was even invented, so we can believe the latter would sacrifice himself for the other. It's also dramatically satisfying as we don't know whether it's because Christie feels responsible for him (Vriess is disabled), or because they are a couple. It could be read either way, or as both.

IN A NUTSHELL: Stock characters are created within communities of real people and can present an opportunity for writers, but only if we build on them and place them in scenarios target audiences do not expect.

MARY SUES AND GREAT WHITE HOPES

Some stock characters seem to exist solely in stories, with little connection to real life at all. For example, I doubt very much you will have heard someone calling a woman a 'Mary Sue' in your day-to-day life. A 'Mary Sue' comes from the fan fiction community (think Wattpad, Kindle Worlds, AsianFanFics, et al.). This is where fans of a particular story, character, celebrity, franchise or storyworld come together and write stories set in those universes. A 'Mary Sue' is a derogatory term for a young, female character – especially a protagonist – who is considered one-dimensional and overly idealised with hackneyed mannerisms. She is often accused of being a stand-in for the story's (usually female) author.

If this term seems vaguely familiar, it's because outspoken Hollywood screenwriter and filmmaker Max Landis launched an attack on Rey, the protagonist of *Star Wars: The Force Awakens*, and called her a 'Mary Sue'. This set the internet alight, for two reasons: men's rights activists (MRAs) felt justified in their boycott of the movie, plus fans – particularly female ones – claimed it was totally unfair and sexist that the Jedi powers that exalted Luke Skywalker to the status of a hero in the original movies were not applied to Rey. To this day, the argument rumbles on, online.

Another tag you will probably have heard of is Great White Hope or White Saviour. Though this exists in real life, too, it's unclear where exactly it started – on the page or in society. The Great White Hope refers to a white character, usually male, who goes to save a group of people of colour from their plight, which may be other white people, a lack of education, or even dragons and monsters. Hollywood in particular is in love with this trope, but versions exist in novels and TV. (TV drama loves to displace a more educated hero and put him or her in a rural community, for example.) Notable Great White Hope stories include *Dances with Wolves* (1990), *Dangerous Minds* (1996), *The Last Samurai* (2003) and *Avatar* (2009) – and these are just for starters!

Audiences have made it very clear where they stand with the Great White Hope character, however – they're bored with it. Even just the suggestion of such a character is enough to condemn a movie in advance. When *The Great Wall* (2017) came out, set in China but starring Matt Damon, Twitter made its feelings very clear with the satirical hashtag #ThankyouMattDamon, in which Damon was thanked not only for saving China, but other things such as teaching individual twitterati how to use chopsticks! This is unsurprising, given Twitter's fierce reputation for social justice, but also because Damon has been a fierce critic of diverse characters in the past. (Incidentally, some critics have posited that *The Great Wall* may not deserve such opprobrium, as Damon's character is not the 'traditional' White Saviour the film's posters make him appear to be. Watch the movie and decide for yourself.)

As ever, the main issue with Great White Hopes is just how many stories exist in this vein. As a result, it would seem the only 'true' hero is the white guy, and that all native or indigenous communities are hapless and doomed until he turns up. Bleurgh.

IN A NUTSHELL: Remember that giving a main character a complimentary role is not the ticket to automatic 'good' characterisation. Concentrate instead on how yours are different from the 'norm' – and ensure they are not flat and stereotypical, to avoid falling back on boring stock characters like the Great White Hope by accident.

ARCHETYPES

Now we've waded through the characterisation 'noise' favoured by social media, this is a good time to think about archetypes. The term 'archetype' has its origins in ancient Greek. The root words are *archein*, which means 'original' or 'old', and *typos*, which means 'pattern', 'model' or 'type'. Those who have studied psychology will know Carl Jung used this term in his work on the psyche, saying there are certain 'types' of people, falling into 12 broad categories:

1. The Hero
2. The Lover
3. The Explorer
4. The Ruler
5. The Innocent
6. The Regular Guy/Gal
7. The Caregiver
8. The Rebel
9. The Creator
10. The Jester
11. The Sage
12. The Magician

He argued that we understand these categories instinctively, because this knowledge is part of human beings' collective unconscious. Whether you believe Jung or think it's a load of cobblers, there is a certain authenticity to the idea of 'types' of people. We all know people we could place under these headings quite easily, plus, the better we know them, the more likely we are to mix and cross over the categories.

It's not hard to see, then, that it's the same with good characterisation: truly great characters don't exist under just one heading. Also, as we've already established, certain genres and types of story have an overflow of certain types of character, but maybe not enough of another kind. As examples, Heroes are frequently Lovers and Explorers and, in recent times, often Jesters and Rebels, too. In the Hero's storyworld, an antagonist will frequently be a Ruler, perhaps a Creator as well. Female characters will frequently be Innocent and/or Caregivers.

At grassroots level, there's nothing wrong with any of this, but most of it is stale and overdone. This is where your research of what's gone before can really help in creating a diverse character, because you will be able to pinpoint what's missing. Sometimes just a tiny change is sufficient; other times, a radical overhaul is necessary. Most of the time, it's somewhere in-between.

IN A NUTSHELL: Target audiences want diverse characters who feel fresh, but also relevant and authentic. Pinpointing what is missing from the produced and published content in your genre or subgenre can help you create a truly diverse character, as it will ensure you remain 'left of the middle' rather than going OTT and creating a character who comes 'out of left field'.

'CLASSIC HEROES' AND DIVERSITY

Classic heroes, or rather those guys (and gals!) who sweep in and save the day from tyrants and despots, are endlessly popular because their stories are easy to understand. Whether you're a small child, an elderly person, or literally grew up poles apart, chances are you know this story. Culture, education, class, age, gender, race – you name it. We pretty much ALL know this story. It is global. It is universal.

When it comes to the hero archetype, writers don't have to dig deep before they come across Joseph Campbell's *Hero with a Thousand*

Faces, particularly his 'monomyth' idea. Christopher Vogler explored this, too, in his own book, *The Hero's Journey*. In both books, the monomyth, or the Hero's Journey, refers to the template of a broad category of tales that involve a hero going on an adventure, winning a victory in a decisive crisis, and then coming home changed or transformed. There are lots of interpretations and versions (including a Heroine's Journey!), but at base level, the idea is:

One hero = LOTS of <u>different</u> tellings of that 'same' story

This is broadly correct and what audiences want, whether they're watching a movie or TV show, or reading a novel. Audiences want a man – or woman! – to go on some sort of quest or mission and, generally speaking, they want him (or her) to be successful. Generally speaking, the audience may want the hero/ine to be changed or transformed in some way by the quest or mission. In addition, this quest or mission may or may not be literal; it may be metaphorical. It may be both.

Now, the Hero's Journey template may not be suitable for ALL stories, genres or types of tales, but it's interesting how many it can be applied to, regardless of medium. Most stories revolve around a kind of problem (or quest or mission) and the protagonist's goal or need is usually to solve it, with the antagonist getting in his/her way for some reason. Most protagonists DO learn something in the course of the narrative, which will probably 'transform' them (or at least their worldview). The secondary characters, then, help or hinder the protagonist or antagonist in their respective goals.

But, while we all know this story at base level, the issue is not with the notion of a hero. We don't need to reinvent the wheel here; the monomyth is what audiences want. Instead, the problem lies in modern heroes' current homogenisation. He – sometimes she – looks the same, acts the same, comes from the same place/storyworld.

IN A NUTSHELL: There are not ENOUGH *different tellings* of the monomyth. In short, when it comes to classic heroes, guess what? We need more diversity to revive this classic character role function.

ANTI-HEROES

When writers write of heroism and the monomyth, then, the character is nearly always male. These notions of masculinity and heroism seem interlinked, along with the notion of 'worth', the idea being that heroes are automatically 'good guys'. But, of course, this isn't true, hence the idea of the 'anti-hero'. Some of our favourite characters are anti-heroes, male leads so flawed, bad even, we can't help but invest in their journey. A cult favourite like this would be our unnamed narrator in Chuck Palahniuk's *Fight Club*, adapted by Jim Uhls for the David Fincher film in 1999: 'I think *Fight Club* did so well in finding its audience because it tapped into the frustrations and resentments of young men, the "toxic masculinity" we hear so much about today,' says Jim.

I totally agree. *Fight Club* was way ahead of its time: if Palahniuk were to write the book today, perhaps the technology would change – in my mind's eye I can see Tyler Durden broadcasting live via Facebook or Snapchat in a balaclava – but overall, the story content would be strikingly similar. Again, that 'Holy Grail' of relatability and relevance hit its mark... and has remained current, some 20 years on. It's said that Palahniuk wrote *Fight Club* during a period when he was feeling frustrated at where his life was going; it was a call to arms to all young men, and why not? As a writer, finding your own truth and being completely unapologetic about it can really help in finding your audience.

IN A NUTSHELL: Anti-heroes can be as powerful as the good guys. But don't make them bad or mad for the sake of it. Find that authentic rage and push it out.

SUPERHEROES

So, writers, unsurprisingly, are keen on trying to tell their own versions of the Hero's Journey, but there are many traps they can fall into. If they don't see what has gone before and consider how they can twist this familiar character, they can end up influenced by the saturation of samey content that surrounds them, especially when it comes to superhero narratives. As a result, 'super' or not, spec heroes will follow the same boilerplate kind of template. The hero will often be tortured and angsty, though endlessly sexual, possibly quite funny, certainly irascible. This was great and expected by audiences for a long time, probably 30 years or so, but now they are bored with it.

The epitome of this type of hero character in produced content is probably Wolverine, especially when he is up against his deadly love interest Jean Grey. While I've never followed the comics, the majority of movies in which this character appears make him the lone wolf who follows that template spec screenwriters in particular are so in love with. He's sexy, angsty, irascible and impossibly strong (invincible, in fact). This is unsurprising: we have nearly two decades of Wolverine movies, all of which fell squarely in the time in which audiences wanted to see that type of hero.

When it comes to diversity, we can see change in action when it comes to Wolverine. It's no accident, then, that the most recent, *Logan* (2017), paints Wolverine in a very different light – so much so, the movie is titled with his first name. But in the storyworld set in 2029, mutants are becoming extinct. Logan is now a carer for the increasingly frail Professor X. He is as irascible and angsty as ever, but seeing him taking the Professor to the toilet, or carrying him upstairs to his room, gives us an insight into his humanity we rarely glimpsed in the franchise before. Even so, frustration and a sense of duty is there – as Professor X declares at the beginning of the movie to Logan, 'You're waiting for me to die.'

This 'softer' side of Logan is not extended to Laura – Wolverine's clone and 11-year-old 'daughter' – for approximately two-thirds of the film. It's clear Laura doesn't need his help anyway. With claws on her hands and feet (thanks to being a girl!), she can fight her way out of most battles. In fact, Logan leaves her behind or attempts to get rid of her repeatedly throughout the movie, only making peace with his fatherly status at the lookout post when he's safely delivered her to the other mutant children. So, when he runs to catch up and save the children from the Reavers, it's his choice, rather than his duty.

IN A NUTSHELL: Even with these changes, Logan is still Wolverine. We are still treated to his trademark roar, his fighting prowess, his tendency to hit the booze. The movie has everything the average *X-Men* fan could want: epic set pieces, some humour, some gore. It's his relationships that set him apart from previous incarnations of this character.

GENDER-FLIPS

With that 'classic' hero so popular across all mediums, it wasn't long before he was gender-flipped, and this is most obvious in movies again. That template came into play with a vengeance in the nineties with the work of James Cameron, with sheroes finding themselves in the same kind of boat (though, intriguingly, they're rarely irascible or even unpleasant, as male heroes like Wolverine are wont to be). Their sexuality is key, like the male hero's, though, interestingly, this is frequently put under greater scrutiny by commentators who don't seem to notice the so-called 'female gaze' as much as the male. This is despite typical sheroes – or Kick-ass Hotties, as I call 'em – usually holding on to more clothes. Sheroes are much more likely to be seen fighting in their underwear (or very scant clothing). It's unlikely we will see their bare breasts or bottoms, for example, whereas the likes of Wolverine will frequently be full-on naked. Full-frontal nudity for male heroes is usually out, but we will see their bare butts with regularity... and occasionally an accidental dong will make it through (yes, *Deadpool*, I'm looking at yours).

Kick-ass Hotties don't tend to sustain franchises in as high numbers as male characters, it seems, but one obvious exception would be Alice in the *Resident Evil* franchise. In a post-apocalyptic world besieged by zombies, Alice is a genetically modified and super-strong 'weapon'. As the franchise goes on, she's probably a clone, too, since we can't be sure we're even dealing with the 'original' Alice. The shady Umbrella Corporation not only caused the zombie infestation, it created Alice, too. The storyworld's roots are very much in *Frankenstein*, and while the movies all seem like demented pop videos, they are great fun (IF you like that sort of thing).

Now, I can't pretend I haven't enjoyed some (if not most) of the content the likes of Wolverine and Alice have appeared in. However, they're pretty dull after nearly 20 years! Even Hugh Jackman and Milla Jovovich are hanging up their hats and calling it a day in 2017. Adaptations of bestselling graphic novels like *The X-Men* and movies based on video games like *Resident Evil* will always make money, so we can probably expect to see more from Wolverine and Alice, albeit with different actors and crews. But it's BECAUSE of this you shouldn't model your own heroes on them!

IN A NUTSHELL: The marketplace already has the good-looking, highly sexual, white, kick-ass hero – male or female – covered. They are everywhere! If you want to write a hero who saves the day, there's no reason you can't. But you DO need to think 'left of the middle' when it comes to characterisation... and this is where diversity comes into play.

MAD MAX: FURY ROAD

As we've already considered in the first section of the book with Gillian Flynn's *Gone Girl*, doing something controversial and 'not the norm' with your characters can be a great shortcut to standing out. Just as many thinkpieces were being penned about the iconic Amy Dunne – both for AND against the book and movie – another story found itself in the internet's firing line in 2015.

As a franchise, *Mad Max* was always seen as full of testosterone, so when MRAs decried the latest instalment, *Mad Max: Fury Road*, as 'feminist propaganda', this seemed unlikely. After all, in the history of epic blockbusters, female characters have largely been sidelined as love interests or the occasional Kick-ass Hottie, especially in action movies. Yet the MRAs called for a boycott of the film, claiming that the story had changed beyond all recognition from the original movies. They even insisted the film wasn't even Max's story; that it was about 'a bunch of women' (the HORROR!).

Now, I was always going to see *Mad Max: Fury Road*, regardless of whose story it was. As a lifelong action fan I loved the original franchise as a girl and had been looking forward to seeing this instalment (especially as I had previously met a stuntman who'd done some work on it and told me some hair-raising tales about the filming out in Nairobi). I couldn't wait!

The MRAs were right about one thing, though: it IS Furiosa's story. If it seems strange that this is such a big deal, consider this: in nearly 40 years of blockbusters, large casts of women grabbing back their own destinies from male control are practically non-existent. That said, though it might be Furiosa's story, *Mad Max: Fury Road* is told via Max's POV; it is framed around him. Essentially a chase movie, the film is much more than that on a subtexual level. This was exciting for me, as I couldn't remember many blockbusters that were as richly layered as this one; often I feel as if I'm overthinking various Hollywood movies I see, but that wasn't the case here. That said, it works on a surface level, too: if you want to view it as 'just' a chase movie, you can quite easily do so. The executive producer on *Mad Max: Fury Road*, Iain Smith, told me writer/director George Miller never set out to make a 'feminist movie' – he wanted something thematic, mythic, and Furiosa was the character who captured his imagination.

All this being said, Max was not surplus to requirements. His appearance in the story wasn't purely about greenlighting a film with six female characters in the lead roles. Had he been missed out altogether, something would have been sorely lacking from the tale. More on why, next.

MAX HIMSELF

On the surface, then, Max Rockatansky is no different from the average hero. He's good-looking and straight, even to the point of having the obligatory dead wife and child (though, to be fair, the original *Mad Max* film set this character trope in motion back in 1979!). Max is the classic 'lone wolf' hero found originally in Westerns, which, over the last 30 to 40 years, has also found its way into blockbuster action-adventures and thrillers of varying types, both epic and urban.

This time around, Max is played by Tom Hardy rather than Mel Gibson, who is now in his sixties. Though writer/director George Miller has claimed *Fury Road* is a sequel to *Mad Max: Beyond Thunderdome* (1985), he's also said it's set '40 years next Wednesday'(!). Miller has also hinted that Hardy's Max *may* be the original man's son, or even a clone. Wherever *Fury Road* is on the timeline, and whether the two Maxes are related by blood or created in a lab, this seems to make a kind of sense: Hardy and Gibson are both good-looking white men of similar size and shape (at least on-screen), with comparable facial attributes. Hardy also brings the 'lone wolf' aspect of the character from the original to his interpretation of the role.

But this is where the similarity ends. In contrast to Gibson's blue-eyed, movie-star good looks (marking him out for Hollywood stardom from the off), Hardy is more of a character actor. Mel Gibson was always a good actor, but in later films he was 'Mel Gibson as...' A star himself, Hardy is still known first and foremost for his body of 'worthy' theatre, television and movie work as he joins the franchise (whereas Gibson, on the other hand, would go on to become a 'proper' filmmaker, before his much publicised disgrace and subsequent comeback).

In terms of actual character content, Hardy's Max is much quieter, lacking the quips and irascible nature of the original Max. The original Max was a policeman before the fall of society and this authoritarian air follows him through all three of the original movies. This means Gibson's Max likes the trappings of the fallen society, so he loves his guns and motorbikes.

In contrast, Hardy's Max is more opportunistic, feral. He will fight with weapons or hands and feet; he doesn't care. He doesn't make allowances – he'll take what he wants and needs to survive. He doesn't have a favourite gun or weapon; he'll kill his enemies by whatever means he can. He's living in the world of men, where there is no hope; he is on the edge of existence. We meet Max peeing, covered in a tangled mass of hair, eating a live lizard. *Fury Road*'s executive producer Iain Smith warns, 'The film opens in the world of testosterone. This is what happens when you have too much of the masculine.'

Unlike many 'lone wolf' heroes of the same ilk, this Max is what I call a 'reluctant hero'. Hardy's Max is passive, defensive. He doesn't want to rescue anyone, which is at complete odds with his hero status – but unlike previous heroes who've said this, Max acts like it, too. According to Iain Smith, George Miller's inspiration for this incarnation of Max came from silent movies, specifically Buster Keaton in *The General* (1926). Max is effectively asexual, which is interesting because audiences might expect him to be sexual, stealing kisses or eyeing up The Wives, probably even 'getting the girl' at the end.

THE SHORT VERSION: *Mad Max: Fury Road* makes a twist on the 'classic' Hero's Journey: instead of killing the baddies and getting the girl, Max's arc is different. He is a true reluctant hero; his connection with Furiosa is not sexual. More than that: Max must go from being an animal, useful only as a 'blood bag', to becoming human again. Max finds his humanity through helping the women escape their oppressors. He does this at great cost to himself, not because he is a hero, but because it's the right thing to do.

FURIOSA

As noted already, Furiosa is the Change Agent in the story. In the same way Max belongs to a previous time, she is instead symbolic of the hope of a new world order. She is the one who takes the war rig off the road, both literally and as a metaphor for a change of direction and the hope it brings. Iain Smith says, 'Charlize [Theron] made that part; her own story of living with a violent father is reflected in *Mad Max: Fury Road*. Behind all her success, the glitz and glamour, the perfume ads, is that South African fighting girl – that's what powers Furiosa.'

Furiosa is your classic 'male role model': she has earned authority over the War Boys on the rig. This is taken for granted. They are perturbed, but not freaked out, when she takes the war rig off the road. She has the same capabilities as any man: she can fight to the death, yet is effortlessly sexy, too... but again, not in the way audiences expect. Some commentary has praised Charlize Theron for 'getting ugly' for the part of Furiosa. I beg to differ. Furiosa is NOT ugly. Not only does her capability make her attractive, but we can't take our eyes off her, just like the dirty, sweaty heroes with their shirts off, such as John McClane in *Die Hard* (1987). By the end of that movie he's as dirty and sweaty as Furiosa, who's covered in oil like a post-apocalyptic Amazon warrior. Yet we're so accostomed to seeing female characters dressed like The Wives that we perhaps don't recognise Furiosa's raw sexuality and magnetism the way we do John McClane's. (Incidentally, The Wives are Breeders. They look sexy on purpose; it's a common imagery. They all look like models because they are models! But again, writer/director George Miller throws all that away, because it doesn't need saying. This makes it all the more powerful because we can IMAGINE what has happened to these women. If the War Boys treat Max as badly as they do, what the hell would they do to them?)

But regardless of how you feel about Furiosa's looks or whether she's a gender-flipped male character, crucially she is still very much a woman. When she and The Wives go to the Green Place, but discover it is no more, there's a very feminine feeling of loss, because there is no home. This is when Furiosa makes her understandable – but nevertheless, huge – mistake, because she decides they must keep going. She saddles up the motorbikes and tries to lead the women across the Great Emptiness. She is leading them all to their deaths.

But if the feminine element of the story will destroy itself by running, this is where the masculine comes in, symbolised in Max because he recommends confrontation. This is the crucial turning point in the story. Max's essential heroism comes to the fore and he chases after the women, even though he doesn't have to at this point. Remember, at the beginning of the story, Max wanted to be left alone, only engaging when he is attacked and abducted by the War Boys. It was this action by the antagonistic force that catapulted him into the story, whether he liked it or not, cementing the movie in thriller territory. Even after his initial escape, Max doesn't want to get involved with Furiosa or The Wives, either. At first, they are irrelevant to him. He wants the war rig. That's it. When he finds he can't drive it without Furiosa, that's when he relents. Max is forced to compromise, because she won't drive without bringing her friends, whom, crucially, *she* is rescuing, not Max.

But Max confronts Furiosa with the reality that the women's only future lies in returning to the Citadel and confronting the evil there. This is a mythic theme along the lines of 'for evil to triumph let good men do nothing'. They clench hands and, by combining her feminine power with his masculine power, they can overcome anything. At that point, the audience knows instinctively Immortan Joe is doomed.

But even when they all emerge victorious in the desert, Max must still return with the women to the Citadel. Furiosa is weak and wounded, but in a (currently) masculine-driven world, the younger and sick War Boys will not accept Furiosa as their victor without Max raising her hand in the air. But as the cries of acceptance echo through the Citadel, Max reverts to type as the lone wolf and leaves; though, the last time we see him, we are aware of the mutual respect between him and Furiosa.

So, for all the talk online of whether *Mad Max: Fury Road* is a feminist film or not, the answer has to be – NO. It is an 'equalist' film, about how men and women can be victorious if they work together. Just as *Mad Max: Fury Road* would be nothing without Furiosa, Max is a crucial character, too. In this story, you cannot have one without the other, because the film is about the power of feminine AND masculine worldviews, not one or the other.

THE SHORT VERSION: Furiosa is a classic, gender-flipped hero character, male to female. However, unlike previous sheroes, her sexuality comes not from how she looks, but from her capability, not least the way she acts and is perceived by those around her, specifically Max. Furiosa's powerful backstory, particularly her being accepted by the War Boys on her rig, plus her diversity via her robotic arm (an 'upgrade', rather than a disability), gives us an insight into WHO she is and HOW she's survived until now in a world of men. She is much, much more than a simple Kick-ass Hottie.

IMMORTAN JOE

Immortan Joe, again at surface level, is a 'classic' villain. Old and ugly, he makes the worst of himself purposefully, to intimidate and strike awe and fear into his underlings. There is a sequence in which Immortan Joe is 'dressed' backstage at the Citadel: with his long, snow-white hair, barrel chest and white make-up spread all over his body, he is hideous, making the women in the audience shudder. To crown this vision, he needs a respirator to breathe, which has been decorated with the face of a monster. Played by Hugh Keays-Byrne (the Toe Cutter in the original *Mad Max*, back in 1979), there could be something comical about him... if not for the fact he has so much power.

Immortan Joe, along with cars and gasoline, is revered in this storyworld. We see the War Boys fawn over him, wanting his acknowledgement; they are prepared to commit jihad in his name, just so they can be 'shiny and chrome'. (It's a sad fact that the War Boys are just cannon fodder here, just as the women are Immortan Joe's property.) The fact that the women on the rig are referred to as Immortan Joe's wives is ludicrous at best. He has no respect for women, their children, or people in general. He cares only about himself and his power. When heavily pregnant Angharad shields Max, Furiosa and the others by hanging defiantly from the rig as it races away (knowing the War Boys will be stopped from firing at her), Immortan Joe bellows, 'That's my property!'

What makes Immortan Joe so effective a villain is that we recognise all his actions from the real world. Even within the free world today, there ARE tyrants and despots who claim to love women and girls and who supposedly want to cherish them, but consistently cut provision for them. To add insult to injury, these men will insist it's 'for women's own good', as if to be female is not to be trusted. Immortan Joe and his ilk literally believe this. We may even know of men who create this situation in miniature within their own homes. We've heard about slave owners of the past calling their slaves 'property', rather than people; this enables them to treat them as little more than animals, trained monkeys in effect – and let's not forget this applies to the War Boys as well. No one in this storyline does well, male or female... only those men in charge. This brings to mind George Orwell's notion of 'some are more equal than others' from *Animal Farm* (1945).

So Immortan Joe is that mythic, evil figurehead. He surrounds himself with brutes and yes-men, who are all more than keen to help him establish his world order. He even has his favourite sons in his inner circle, because they are his most fervent believers. Living in the desert, Immortan Joe keeps mutiny at bay by controlling the water supply and delivering bombastic speeches, like the ones Hitler was infamous for. When Joe and his entourage set off in pursuit of Furiosa and the war rig, he takes with him drummers, bringing to mind tribal war patterns. The 'Doof Warrior' is the star of these sequences, suspended from wires like a mannequin, playing furious and threatening riffs as a form of psychological warfare against their targets. Again, this tactic comes directly from real life! During World War Two, American soldiers travelling by foot through Europe would play mournful scales on their harmonicas in order to freak out retreating German troops up ahead. During the Vietnam War, American helicopters would blare out Wagner's 'Ride of the Valkyries' into the jungle (that's the tune for Looney Toons' famous 'Kill the Rabbit' with Bugs Bunny versus Elmer Fudd for anyone under 40). Again, seemingly comical – yet very effective when trying to break your enemy's resolve.

THE SHORT VERSION: The best and most effective villains are those whose actions we can recognise from real life. Villains are no more the sum of how they look than heroes are. Understanding the psychology and tactics of tyrants, dictators, politicians and even 'ordinary' men and women who've done terrible things is key in enabling audiences to connect with bad characters.

CHARACTERISATION VERSUS PLOT

There's much deliberation in the writing community about which comes first: character or plot. Some writers will create a character, then think about the types of things that may or may not have happened to him or her. Others – including Stephen King, incidentally, in his 2000 memoir *On Writing* – say they distrust plot, but think instead about the 'situation' (which seems the same thing to me, to be honest). Many writers call this the 'What if...?' question, which the story – including its characters – grows from.

Personally, I don't think it matters which method you prefer. You may even find yourself doing a combination of the two things, for different projects or even at the same time. As I discuss with my Bang2writers and script-editing clients, all that really matters is for writers to understand that characterisation and plot are inextricably linked. In the best stories, these two things not only underpin the narrative, they cannot be separated. If you can separate character and plot too easily and find yourself saying '...or there would be no story', you have an issue! The way I view characterisation and plot is very simple and, for me, covers all stories and all mediums:

BEGINNING

- A protagonist has a problem, so wants or needs something to deal with that

MIDDLE

- The protagonist decides to solve the problem despite the obstacles (i.e. the antagonist)

- Things get worse (probably because of the antagonist and various other obstacles)
- The protagonist starts to solve the problem (the antagonist starts to lose, and/or the obstacles begin to recede)

END

- Protagonist (usually) solves the problem, defeats the antagonist and overcomes the obstacles

THE SHORT VERSION: If it looks straightforward, that's because it is! We're not reinventing the wheel here. We know all this stuff! As I've mentioned, it's universal and it's deeply engrained: even small children can tell stories with beginnings, middles and ends. All you have to choose is WHO your characters will be and HOW you're going to plot it.

SEVEN BASIC PLOTS

Storytelling isn't just about heroes 'saving the day', nor overt good versus evil. Just as one size should not fit all for diverse characters, there are plenty of stories that do not fit the Hero's Journey mould. Influenced by Jung's work, Christopher Booker wrote a book called *The Seven Basic Plots* (2004), summarising the broad categories of stories available to writers, which he listed as:

- **Overcoming the Monster.** Horror is an obvious choice here: franchises featuring creatures like *Alien*'s Xenomorph or more human monsters, as in *Halloween*, *Friday the 13th* and more recently *Saw*, fall under this banner. But various versions of the thriller and action-adventure story can mine this plot, too. As characters will probably fear for their lives in this storyline, sometimes the monster in question will be a terrible regime. The dystopian subgenre of YA is well versed in this plot, with modern offerings like *The Hunger Games*, but so is 'spec fic' meant for more adult audiences, as in Margaret Atwood's 1987 classic *The Handmaid's Tale*.

- **Rags to Riches.** Taking its cue from fairy tales like *Cinderella*, family animations and children's stories use this plot the most, transposing those fairy tales or using them as a springboard. This storyline may cross over with comedy, or rebirth, as in some books, TV shows and movies inspired by true events, like *Three Kings* (1999), in which three American soldiers caught up in the 1991 Gulf War steal Iraqi gold. Just as often, the plot may be reversed in this latter version, too, as we watch a character's downfall. Sometimes a character may turn this around a second time and thwart the expected ending, as in 2011's *Limitless*; other times s/he may die, such as in *The Place Beyond the Pines* (2012).

- **The Quest.** Immediately we can see the Hero's Journey as fitting very neatly in this category. Certainly, if we consider Greek myths like Homer's *Odyssey*, most Quest stories since seem to fill this template. If you were a small child in the eighties like I was, you will remember Quest stories were everywhere, especially in movies featuring fantasy and muppets like *Labyrinth* (1986), *The NeverEnding Story* and *Legend* (both 1985). Modern children's movies have sought to emulate this, too, with Pixar, Dreamworks and Disney having characters undertaking missions to find objects and people and save the day, such as 2016's *Trolls*.

- **Voyage and Return.** In classic fiction like *Alice in Wonderland* (1865) by Lewis Carroll and H.G. Wells's *The Time Machine* (1895), a protagonist goes to a strange land and then returns with that experience. If heroes most frequently go on quests, it can create a new opportunity if you have them do something else. Compared to the likes of *Labyrinth*, it's immediately apparent that *Mad Max: Fury Road* is – unusually – a 'voyage and return' story. Max ends up in the strange, nightmarish world of Immortan Joe and the War Boys against his will. Furiosa attempts to escape that world with The Wives, ending up with Max quite by accident.

Ironically, all of them must return and make a stand in order to be free, but they can only do this by beating Immortan Joe out on the road. In other words, Max and Furiosa would never have been victorious if they had stayed at the Citadel. They have to make the journey and combine their respective forces in order to go back.

- **Comedy.** Shakespeare is, of course, the comedy king, but there is a rich history in this genre covering all mediums. Booker stresses comedy goes 'beyond' just telling jokes. Instead, he says it's about specific light, humorous characterisation and tone, which must end with a happy or cheerful ending. 'Feelgood' films would fall under comedy, as would most romances. This is a little problematical in terms of categorisation in my opinion, because what about subgenres like black comedy, very dark satire and horror comedy? (I guess, though, even when the gross-out or fear factor is high, especially in more flamboyant offerings like *Tremors* (1990), *Shaun of the Dead* (2004) and *Cabin in the Woods* (2011), the mood is still 'light' in that there's a sense of hope or irony at the end, even if the body count is high.)

- **Tragedy.** Again, Shakespeare had this plot type covered, with the likes of *King Lear*, *Romeo and Juliet* and *Macbeth* and their many adaptations across all mediums. What really makes a tragedy is not sad stuff happening – though that obviously helps – but the fact that the protagonist has a fatal flaw of some kind which ultimately leads to their downfall (this sometimes overlaps with a 'rags to riches' story, especially when combined with a true story, as in *Bonnie and Clyde*, 1967). In recent years, dramas on both TV and film, plus literary and women's fiction, have mined the tragedy plotline.

- **Rebirth.** In this plotline, an important event or happening forces the main character to change their ways, often making the character a better person. This storyline sometimes features anti-heroes, probably inspired by the likes of Scrooge from Charles Dickens's *A Christmas Carol* (1843). This story – not to mention its many adaptations – means children's stories like *Dr Seuss' How the*

Grinch Stole Christmas and Dreamworks' *Despicable Me* find their target audiences immediately.

There is a smattering of TV anti-heroines, such as *Nurse Jackie* (2009–15) and Nancy from *Weeds* (2005–12), but in movies, intriguingly, anti-hero protagonists are nearly always male. Notable exceptions include anti-heroines who may be true-life figures, such as P.J. Travers in *Saving Mr Banks* (2013) or Aileen Wuornos in *Monster* (2003). From books, my favourite anti-heroine protagonist was always Mary Lennox from *The Secret Garden* (1911) by Frances Hodgson Burnett. She's selfish, rude, inconsiderate. It's a little boy, the sick and sidelined Colin, who will show Mary the error of her ways. If written today, it might have been written the other way around with the gender of the protagonist and secondary reversed, as female characters are so often expected to be 'positive' or 'role models'.

THE SHORT VERSION: Most genres and types of story across all mediums can be boiled down into just a few plots. This has a knock-on effect on characterisation, because we end up with the same kinds of characters in the same kinds of stories. But what if writers paid more attention to this and transplanted these characters into DIFFERENT types of stories? What would we gain in terms of diversity?

TWO MORE PLOTS?

Some commentators also add 'Rebellion Against the One' and 'Mystery' to these seven basic plots. I disagree with the former and agree with the latter (though you must weigh up the evidence and decide for yourself). In the first instance, I see very little difference between 'The One' and 'The Monster' – whether protagonists vanquish a literal beast or a metaphorical one (such as Immortan Joe), I think it's essentially the same story. I think adding 'Rebellion Against the One' is essentially splitting hairs.

'Mystery', however, is an intriguing addition and one that appeals to me personally as a crime fiction writer and avid reader of mysteries.

'Whodunit' brings forth a rich history of stories in which a detective character – amateur sleuth or professional – must solve a problem and bring equilibrium back to the storyworld. Authors like Agatha Christie excelled at this and put this story on the map, so it seems strange not to include it. In recent years, particularly post-2010 with *Gone Girl*, the 'whydunit' has increased in popularity, too; the mystery is not so much who has committed the crime, but WHY. This frequently asks readers – and viewers – to relate to antagonists, or even protagonists who have committed terrible acts.

IN A NUTSHELL: The whodunit and whydunit have become increasingly popular, especially in the last 100 years in the post-Agatha Christie age. This has spread from books, to TV, to films.

MAKING YOUR OWN HERO OR VILLAIN

Regardless of whether you're writing a novel or screenplay, if you know what 'type' of character you want to write and what role function they should perform (and why), you can draw your inspiration from whatever published and produced content you like. If you want, then, to write a classic hero protagonist and a vile villain in an epic, sprawling storyworld, why not check out some of the many, many stories that have come out of Hollywood in the last 30 or 40 years? You need only ask one question, though there are many possibilities:

WHAT IF **YOUR** HERO OR VILLAIN WAS...

- **...Not white?** The likes of Will Smith and Vin Diesel have played classic heroes in the action-adventure and thriller genres. Vin Diesel has also played anti-hero Riddick, plus Chiwetel Ejiofor made a star-making turn as The Operative, the complex villain in Joss Whedon's *Serenity* (2005). Zoe Saldana has played the action heroine, but she is unusual when white stars like Angelina

Jolie, Cameron Diaz, et al. usually take on this role. In the nineties, when I was growing up, there seemed to be more East Asian heroes than there are now: Jackie Chan, Jet Li, Lucy Liu. Like their white counterparts, BAME heroes and heroines are usually funny, capable, irascible, effortlessly cool. But what if they were slightly *different*, somehow? How could their heritage help or hinder them in their mission or quest?

- **...Gender-flipped?** Furiosa in *Mad Max: Fury Road* has more in common with male heroes than female ones. She is dirty, sweaty, covered in oil, with a shaved head. She literally doesn't give a shit how she looks. It's her capability and sheer power that attract audiences to her. It's getting harder and harder to gender-flip characters now – Hollywood in particular has been doing this in earnest for three decades – but it can be done if you find a 'way in' like this; it's not enough merely to swap genders.

- **...LGBT?** More recent discussions of LGBT issues have prompted some to refer to it as LGBTQ, adding 'queer' to the acronym. Could Max in *Fury Road* come under 'Q', if we take 'queer' to incorporate asexuality? Whatever the case, Max is not interested in sex, but survival. It's a tiny change, but makes for a much more diverse character when literally every other male hero is gagging for it! But where are the gay, bisexual and trans heroes, especially male ones? Again, research can help writers find a possible way in: the Sacred Band of Thebes military unit in Ancient Sparta was said to be made up of same-sex couples. It was thought the Spartans were motivated and even more heroic as a result of their homosexual romantic bonds with one another. Why not?

- **...Disabled?** Antagonists are frequently disabled or disfigured, leading some activists to believe storytellers are making a moral judgement. However, if disability forms part of your storyworld as a whole (as it always has done in the *Mad Max* franchise), this neatly removes this possible connection. Just as vile villain Immortan Joe has a disability, so does Furiosa; many other characters do, too, as is especially evident in crowd scenes. Iain Smith adds, 'Disabled people tell me they love the storyworld of *Mad Max* because we don't make much of (disability). These are the characters' stories; this is their lives. That's it.'

HANNIBAL THE CANNIBAL AND PSYCHOPATHY

Probably the most well-known antagonist of all time is Hannibal Lecter. He's so memorable that even if someone has never read a book or seen a movie or TV episode with him in, they know 'what' he is – 'Hannibal the Cannibal' is a striking and clever epitaph to remember him by. Hannibal is a psychopath AND a psychiatrist, which means he is both animalistic and highly educated. He is also an authority figure, yet has somehow managed to evade capture for indulging his baser desires.

Hannibal is a contradiction in terms, which is what makes him so fascinating. This is why the character broke new ground when he first came to the public's attention, especially via the Oscar-winning horror film, *The Silence of the Lambs* (1991). We've spent the past 25 (plus) years obsessed with him, with various other books, films and TV shows about him and how he came to 'be'.

But antagonists like Hannibal Lecter are pure fantasy. As crime author Rosie Claverton – herself a psychiatrist – points out: 'So, how does Hannibal hold down a job as a psychiatrist AND eat people so regularly??' The average psychopath has limited intelligence, plus the self-control necessary to deny such extreme bloodlust would mean it unlikely anyone could pass as 'a wolf in sheep's clothing' for long. Historically, we can consider such serial killers as Ted Bundy here: a clever man, he was still unable to stop himself revealing his murderous tendencies again and again, even breaking into a sorority house and killing the trainee nurses there, much the way a fox breaks into a hen house and wreaks havoc. If you read a lot about serial killers – and, as a crime author, I do – it would seem such flamboyant killers feel compelled to reveal themselves.

Psychopathy should not be mistaken for psychosis – another mistake writers make frequently. A psychopath – like Lecter – lacks the ability to love or establish meaningful relationships, often because he's obsessed with control and punishment. He may also fail to learn from experience due to his own ego (and psychopaths are most often male). Pyschiatrists have recently posited there may be little difference between psychopaths and sociopaths (apart from the name); traditionally, 'sociopath' refers to an anti-social personality disorder, characterised by criminality, cruelty or manipulation (though not necessarily murder or even physical violence). In comparison, psychosis relates to a severe mental disorder that can strike anyone, regardless of gender: thoughts and emotions become so impaired the sufferer loses contact with reality (and is often struck with fear, self-loathing and/or anger).

Yet many writers will not know the difference, writing instead the versions they've seen in newspapers, rather than doing proper research into mental illness. The most common description of the 'knife-wielding psycho' trope I see is that the character is a 'paranoid schizophrenic'. Yet it's extremely unusual for a paranoid schizophrenic to be violent towards others; this is society myth-making, taken straight from lurid tabloid pages.

Lastly, it's worth remembering there is only one Hannibal Lecter. Because of the history of this character, I see a lot of deeply intelligent, authoritarian serial killers in the spec screenplays and unpublished novels I read. But that's been done! If writers want to break new ground and create new, fresh and authentic antagonists, they need to be more diverse. Don't just copy what has gone before.

IN A NUTSHELL: Hannibal the Cannibal worked back in the eighties because nothing like him had been done before. He has cemented himself in the audience's psyche, but nearly three decades on, we want something new from antagonists. So, if you're going to write a psychopath or similar, make sure you do your research; don't just recycle what you've seen in and absorbed from the tabloids.

A LOOK IN (MY) SPEC PILE

As a script reader, I see many of those 'usual' characters and plots in the spec pile, mostly in screenplays but sometimes in unpublished novels and advanced reading copies (ARCs) as well. To shine a light on this and demystify what I get on a daily basis, I sat down and looked through all my notes and coverage, composing broad storylines with various lead characters in mind. I was shocked by the lack of diversity in types of protagonists and the storyworlds they inhabit, even allowing for the different 'types' of these characters within the broader strokes. Here's what I found:

- **White, male, heterosexual action heroes save the day.** Unsurprisingly, given the emphasis on the Hero's Journey, this guy turns up all the time in the spec pile. He'll save the day and look gorgeous doing it. He's usually in the region of 30 to 40 years old; probably has a dead wife/girlfriend (sometimes an entire family); and he's usually pretty tortured and angsty. He's an expert at what he does – whether that's science or kicking ass (sometimes both!) – and he WILL BE SUCCESSFUL at everything he does. But then, that's never in doubt, especially in an action-adventure or thriller! See also what I term Kick-ass Hotties – this is when writers decide to gender-flip their male hero but don't make her any more three-dimensional. She'll usually have a dead daughter (rarely a dead husband, intriguingly, so presumably she was a single mother before her child died!). Of course, Kick-ass Hottie is also white and heterosexual, though she will usually be a bit younger, in her twenties or early thirties. Some novels do have gay lead characters who act heroically, such as Mari Hannah's *DCI Kate Daniels* series, or Rachel Manija Brown and Sherwood Smith's *Stranger* series, which is YA. On television, Clark in *The 100* (2014) is a female hero with a tortured past and sense of responsibility who is also bisexual; we're far more likely to see bisexual women than men generally. Captain Jack in BBC's *Torchwood* (2006–11) is probably the closest we've come so far to a bisexual male hero on TV. Most male and female LGBT characters who are heroic are more often supporting cast in movies, both produced and spec.

HOW TO FLIP IT: Action heroes need to be less often white as standard (particularly female ones) and need more depth, especially if you want your spec action hero to stand out. Powerful backstories can revive this dull and stale-feeling character, male or female. Just beware of making that backstory about dead wives and children. Maybe think about ethnicity to do this, or disability, which has already been done to some extent. Sexuality, or a trans identity, would probably be the writer's greatest challenge for a hero protagonist across all mediums.

• **Pale, stale males are very sad for some reason.** This guy is usually white again and probably in his early twenties. He may be in a novel or a screenplay (if the latter, it's usually a feature, rather than TV). In his storyline, he may have flashbacks, often to school where he was bullied; or he has issues with his parents, who may have neglected him; sometimes both. He's usually from quite a privileged background and is probably depressed. He'll probably kill himself at the end of the story (by hanging himself), or he will get into a fight where he is killed by someone else (often stabbed). Between the beginning and the end, nothing much happens other than a lot of staring into space. Frequently writers will say they want to talk about mental health issues in young men with this character – a very worthy cause, when we consider suicide is one of the biggest killers of young males in real life – but there needs to be a plot to make us invest in the character's journey. Interestingly, I've not seen as many 'miserable female' narratives, though certain subgenres of women's fiction, both published and unpublished, do suffer from a glut of bored housewives who feel underappreciated by their spouses and children.

HOW TO FLIP IT: A story about mental health and (young) people is long overdue, so a well-thought-out plot could help you bring forth this powerful message or theme. It needs to have significant meat to make it work, so a lot of research would be necessary.

- **Abused woman goes after her oppressors.** Usually a rape/revenge story or based around domestic abuse, a woman will first experience the violence against her, then plan and enact her revenge. It's often extremely thin on plot and nearly always a feature screenplay. However, going from 'victim to victor' could include all manner of character motivations and be a very human story.

  HOW TO FLIP IT: If women are nearly always the ones being abused in movies – and they are – what if your abused woman was an abused man? What if the oppressor was female instead? We're beginning to see this in novels like *A Suitable Lie* by Michael J. Malone (Orenda Books), or on TV, with storylines such as Tyrone's abuse at wife Kirsty's hands in *Coronation Street*.

- **Screwed-up (old) man.** Male protagonists, especially those over the age of 50 (though some younger, too), will often have significant problems like terminal illness. The latter has made a huge splash post-*Breaking Bad*, which is hardly a surprise given the show's success and critical acclaim worldwide. For a long time, nearly all detectives in the spec pile had issues with alcohol, then it was gambling. Most are estranged from the women in their lives (if their wives are not dead or missing). Sometimes these guys will have a daughter – hardly ever a son, for some reason – who will counsel them about moving on, or getting their acts together, especially if it's a kitchen-sink-type TV pilot. Sometimes 'screwed-up old man' will be much younger, somewhere between his twenties and early forties. He'll probably be a dopehead and/or gamer, though usually he is a secondary character, rather than a protagonist.

  HOW TO FLIP IT: Interestingly, I've noted older women don't tend to be cast in this role of being 'screwed up' in the specs I read, yet women in real life also struggle with problems such as addiction. Female characters who have terminal illness in stories are usually brave and stoic, but what if they had 'unfinished business' like these previous spec detectives? Or what if they were angry at their diagnosis and the unfairness of it and NOT willing to 'put up and shut up'?

- **Hitman on the run.** Love them or loathe them, hitmen, mafiosi and gangsters will always be popular with audiences, so it's not difficult to see why there is such a glut of movies about them, and also TV series like *The Fixer* (2008) and *The Equaliser* (1985 –9), remade as a movie with Denzel Washington in 2014. Look on Goodreads and you'll find a variety of novels, too, including the classic *Day of the Jackal* by Frederick Forsyth, or *Crying Freeman* by Kazuo Koike, a graphic novel. As you'd expect, there are plenty of video games in this vein, too, such as the eponymous *Hitman*, or *Assassin's Creed* – not to mention their movie adaptations! Hell, I've even associate-produced one (original) hitman film myself – *Assassin* (2015) – and yes, it sold very well. The notion of a character operating outside of not only the law, but the usual rules, like 'Thou shalt not kill', is very appealing.

  HOW TO FLIP IT: Produced and published hitmen stories will often take on elements of the spy subgenre; or discuss themes of justice, or vigilantism; or mix the conventional elements of a hitman story type with those of another genre. But when a character is SO widespread and well known, there need to be some significant twists on audience expectation for the story to feel fresh. Some characters need to feel 'more diverse' than others to continue to work. The hitman is too often crossed with the 'screwed-up old man' character in the spec pile. Even a gender-flip to an older, female assassin could work (especially when all other female assassins are hot and hardcore). Equally, mixing a hitman story with another genre, such as comedy, would feel fairly fresh in today's climate, when comedy-thriller (as opposed to action-adventure) has been pretty much 'out of fashion' since the eighties.

- **Character improves him/herself for love.** I read a lot of feature-length, rom-com screenplays in which a character must 'shape up' and improve their ways in order to be successful in relationships. In recent years – probably because of the likes of *The 40-Year-Old Virgin* (2005) and *Crazy, Stupid, Love* (2011) – characters in specs are much older, usually late thirties/early forties, and at (what they think is) 'the last-chance saloon' for bagging a partner. There is no room for singledom in these specs' storyworld – dying alone is NOT an option. Male protagonists will need to stop gaming, drinking, shave off their beards and lose weight. They will have to learn better communication skills and largely stand on ceremony every time they are on dates in order to impress women (who would otherwise think they're a slovenly, disappointing, juvenile mess). Female protagonists, in comparison, will have to dial DOWN their achievements. They will have to hide how much money they're making, be less intimidating, be more passive. Of course, over the course of the narrative and no matter the individual ins and outs of each plot, BOTH protagonists will decide to behave as and do what they like, and to hell with romance... which, of course, is when love comes knocking. It would seem the 'Be yourself' message is very much alive and well in the spec screenplay pile!

On one level, spec rom-com screenwriters aren't wrong; the message of most published and produced romance-related content DOES carry the message 'Be yourself'. The idea you should change *just* for a partner and essentially live a lie is repulsive to most people in your potential audience. Instead, it's the HOW that has changed. The notion of relationships 'having' to be geared towards marriage or cohabitation, or even monogamy or 'exclusive' commitments, is long gone. It's largely accepted that relationships can take many forms, as long as the people in them are consenting. If we consider rom-com movies of the last 20 years, we've moved very swiftly from 'happy ever after/ Prince Charming'-type narratives via the Richard Curtis model that started with *Four Weddings and a Funeral* (1994) through to bromance, which places male friendship at the heart of a narrative, like *I Love You, Man* (2009), to more raucous affairs dealing with the awkwardness of falling in love with your friends, as in *Just Friends* (2006) or *Friends with Benefits* (2011). There was even a short segue into what producers called 'anti-rom-com' where the two star-crossed lovers DON'T end up together, such as *(500) Days of Summer* (2009).

HOW TO FLIP IT: Keep the message, ditch the familiar plot. There are loads of ways you could tell this story, so make sure you work out what 'type' yours is and what's gone before, so you can twist those characters and introduce more diversity.

- **Disparate group of (young) people get killed for some reason.** Whether a serial killer comes after them, or they walk unwittingly into a monster's lair, this strand of the horror genre is feeling a bit stale. We know they will die, one by one, because it's been a template in place at least since 1979 with *Alien*. Yet monsters appear to have lost their appeal with horror audiences, as does so-called 'torture porn' in which characters are horribly maimed and mutilated while we look on with voyeuristic disgust and awe. Instead, dread and suspense have been very much back on the horror menu in the last five years. While 'creature features' have become largely thriller-orientated, horror is still a huge draw, especially supernatural horror at the moment, via ghosts and other wicked apparitions like demons, witches and other creatures from hell, largely thanks to the influence of Blumhouse (which was behind such modern classic franchises as *Paranormal Activity*, *Insidious* and *Sinister*).

HOW TO FLIP IT: Mixing the modern and the mythical can really help when it comes to horror. The best horrors have situations in which audiences can relate primal, childish fears to things they may do or use every day: technology; sex; eating; sleeping; even their own homes. Explore subtext and consider moments of silence and dread, as opposed to hysterical running about and shouting.

- **Maverick wo/man fixes problems and/or solves crimes/cases.** Frequently, these are TV pilots and a love letter to the likes of

Doctor Who and *The Sarah Jane Adventures*. Sometimes, it's not one main protagonist, but a dynamic duo, as in *The X Files*. Very often these specs don't stand out because they are wholesale rehashes, though I have seen some with good twists on the 'usual'. In a flooded marketplace, however, even with a good hook, it's still very difficult to get attention for a very expensive TV series like this, especially if you have no previous credits.

HOW TO FLIP IT: Change format! Think seriously about writing it as a novel series, or short films, or a web series of your own. Create a following online for it. Alternatively, why not write a feature with these characters and use it as a calling-card script, or a submission to screenwriting contests?

- **Person gets terminal cancer, learns what's important in life, then dies heroically.** (Can be closely linked with 'inspiration porn', too, as mentioned earlier in this section of the book.) As a cancer survivor myself, this really does my proverbial swede in. Obviously, people are diagnosed – and die – from cancer every day, but did you know that AS MANY people survive cancer as die from it, nowadays? It's even thought it may be more, given that so many of the elderly die 'with' cancer, rather than 'from' it. Now, you may know this already, but many of the writers I work with confess they see cancer as an automatic death sentence, which is why their characters with cancer die, more often than not. This is not surprising: in the Western world, cancer is probably one of our ultimate fears, plus the psychological trauma of the disease (not to mention undergoing treatment) is immense. It's also true that cancer can bestow new worldviews, senses of being or a new appreciation for life in general on those who get it. Yet, as with everything, this predominant view of the disease is OVERDONE! Plus, writers take their ideas about cancer from TV, books or movies more often than they do real, lived experiences, which is why the majority of characters die... because they do in TV, books and movies. Soap operas in the UK have a long history of killing off characters with cancer; in the last three or four years, however, they have started to feature characters surviving cancer prominently in their storylines as well. In *EastEnders*, Tanya survived cervical cancer; in *Emmerdale*, characters Brenda and David survived a brain tumour and testicular cancer respectively. In *Coronation Street*, Sally's breast cancer was something the actress herself was going through – and beat! – in real life. In these depictions, the characters were subjected to the full gamut of emotions, from diagnosis through to treatment and its success: denial, anger, pessimism, optimism – you name it. They also had to deal with their 'normal' lives and issues, too, such as going to work, even when they felt ill, or dealing with their kids' problems. These characters were not saintly or heroic, which was so refreshing and authentic.

HOW TO FLIP IT: Cancer is one of the most (likely) adverse life events we will have to face. Yet in dealing with cancer stories, what if your character was NOT terminal? How would s/he deal with the hand s/he's been dealt? What about having to live with the inevitable changes cancer treatment brings with it, such as surgery, like colostomy bags or mastectomies; or chemotherapy, which may bring with it infertility or hearing loss? Also, what about that strange time AFTER treatment, plus the fears of it coming back? There's so much to mine here in terms of conflict, yet the average character with cancer will do something AMAZING, then wither away and die. Author Paula Daly asserts, 'Let's lose disabled/terminally ill characters who are completely accepting of their situations. There's too much stoic resignation. Make them mad! Make them arseholes. Why not?' Indeed!

- **Period drama famous WAG.** I read a lot of feature biopics about the women in famous men's lives, whether wife or girlfriend (mistress). Whether politician, painter, writer or something else, 'The Wife of X' will offer an alternative view of what that famous guy was really like. I can see why screenwriters think this works, but it feeds into the narrative that women are largely decorative. Certainly, I'd be happy to be proved wrong as I'm sure there's a fascinating story to be mined here. That said, I am bored of reading the various versions I've seen so far that basically go like this: i) WAG gets together with famous guy and everything is great; ii) problems arise and everything goes to hell; iii) she dies or gets discarded/imprisoned… or another bloke sweeps in and rescues her!

HOW TO FLIP IT: What if you told the story of a famous woman from her HUSBAND's point of view? I'm struggling to think of a single time I've seen this in the spec pile. Alternatively, why not do away with the WAG action altogether and focus on the women themselves… yes, please! Don't forget there is a rich history of these types of movies, which have done well at awards ceremonies and at the box office, especially this century, from *Erin Brockovich* (2000) to *Hidden Figures* (2016).

- **Selfish man/woman has to learn the hard way.** In spec rom-coms, a vain man or woman has to 'learn what's important' – usually that money or looks should come second to love. In dramas and dramedies, a man usually loses his wife or girlfriend and has to prove to her he's changed. In some scripts aimed at teenagers, the teenage protagonist has to discover his/her parents only have his/her best interests at heart.

HOW TO FLIP IT: Selfishness is overdone in the spec pile as a 'flaw' in characterisation. Why not pick another emotion or worldview that could govern your character's decisions? Much is made of female characters needing to be 'strong', but what if they were WEAK? Same goes for male characters, too. Human weakness is universal and can lead to all types of problems and confrontations.

- **Selfish man/woman has to improve him/herself to get an inheritance.** As with the previous story, plus the variation in which s/he has to improve for love, this character is offered a lot of money in order to be a 'better person'. This money usually comes in the form of an inheritance offered by a mother or father on their deathbed; sometimes the relative will ensure there are certain obstacles or trials the protagonist must go through to get that money.

HOW TO FLIP IT: Offering money as an incentive to change is always a dodgy place for a protagonist to begin, because society carries the message we should do things for our loved ones literally FOR love, NOT money. However, even when dealing with an anti-hero protagonist (and why not?), we still have a suspension-of-disbelief issue, because WHY has the catalyst parent character waited until being on his/her deathbed before putting this into motion? Yet there is a long history of families banding together to create interventions to help loved ones who have gone off the rails, as we see in *The Dilemma* (2011). So why not begin with an intervention? Where could that take your character?

- **Real-life or literary figure does something surprising and (probably) supernatural.** Like the period drama WAGs, this is a character who appears to turn up again and again in the spec pile, yet very infrequently appears in produced or published content; I can only assume the likes of *Abraham Lincoln: Vampire Hunter* (2012) and *Hansel and Gretel: Witch Hunters* (2013) are responsible! Famous figures from history (particularly literature) will appear as monster hunters, time travellers, or as witches and wizards themselves. These stories will most often be spec TV pilots, where 'stories of the week' will revolve around the solving of crimes, or a rescue. Figures such as Shakespeare, Charles Dickens, Jane Austen and Mary Shelley, plus the entire catalogue of characters from *Grimm's Fairy Tales*, make the most appearances.

HOW TO FLIP IT: As ever, it's difficult to stand out when many writers are doing similar things, involving similar characters. Choosing a historical or literary figure who is NOT Shakespeare, Abraham Lincoln, Jane Austen, Charles Dickens, Mary Shelley or a fairy-tale character could pay dividends. Additionally, a change of format could probably really help. A novel, web series, graphic novel or feature-length screenplay would be a welcome change to a 30–60-page TV pilot.

- **Teen sociopath who's a good lad really.** Nearly always male, this teenager is a 'bad' kid... he'll rob, beat others up, even bully and intimidate. But we discover this is because he has to look after his younger siblings, who've been abandoned – either literally or metaphorically – by a feckless or depressed mother. Dad is never on the scene. Frequently this boy will be rehabilitated by a stable influence, usually an older male or female; or he will fall in with local mafiosi and end up doomed. Sometimes this character will be female, though she is rarely abusive; instead she will be the one who is abused, like a modern-day Cinderella, usually looking after her father and brothers until a Prince Charming-type takes her away from it all.

  HOW TO FLIP IT: Growing up in poverty or as a victim of neglect – or both – human beings may become accustomed to fighting for everything they have, so a teenager acting aggressively is not surprising. Yet we think of aggression as a 'male' trait, so what if a female character was an intimidating bully or wannabe gangster? In contrast, what if your male teenager was subjugated by his family because he wanted a quiet life? Remember the words of author Ali Land (*Good Me Bad Me*) here, when it comes to writing a complex teenage character: 'That combination of agony and arrogance I find really hard to get right – but for some reason I keep trying to climb up the wall.' If you know any teens in the wild, or have one in your home, you know just how ON POINT 'agony and arrogance' is!

- **Millennial girl gets stuck in.** This one seems to have turned up out of nowhere in the spec pile during the last couple of years. Millennial Girl is usually in her early twenties and dissatisfied with her life, plus she's sassy, cool and intelligent – not to mention fiercely feminist. She'll stick her nose into situations where she's not wanted, especially when it comes to figures of authority and cover-ups. We've seen this character in both published and produced content, incarnated by the likes of Freddie in *The Social Media Murders* by Angela Clarke, plus Dory in TV's *Search Party* (who is surely named for *Finding Nemo*!). I think we'll see a large upsurge of Millennial Girl-type characters in the next five years if the spec pile is anything to go by.

HOW TO FLIP IT: This character has been female every time I've read it; she's nearly always straight and able-bodied and white. As time goes on, I will put money on the idea we will see Millennial Boys, plus those with disabilities and from the BAME and LGBT communities, too.

- **Protagonist goes to find him/herself.** Whether they take themselves off to a seemingly mysterious foreign land, or up an icy mountain, our protagonist is probably 'middle-aged' (whatever that means) and white. S/he will be faced with some kind of life-changing trauma – a cancer diagnosis, an accident, a relationship breakdown or a spouse randomly dropping dead – and will feel compelled to 'reconnect with life' somehow. Whether helping a troubled community for some reason, or doing something potentially dangerous, this character will grow spiritually over the course of the narrative. It's a nice idea and not completely inauthentic, but it is dull and overdone. It can also cross over with the similarly overdone 'white saviour' trope, especially when focused on the efforts of white people, male or female. I'm also reminded of another friend of mine who declared when I was talking about this, 'I went to India, you know. About ten years ago, when my marriage broke up. I went for eight months.' I blinked. I hadn't ever known he was married. But I decided to let that one go. 'Did you "find" yourself?' I queried. He grinned. 'No, I was just as confused when I came back as when I left. But I had a fabulous time!'

HOW TO FLIP IT: True stories can be a powerful way of connecting this well-known, human notion of 'finding yourself' with a diverse character. Stories of adoption and searches for biological parents are an obvious choice for characters who want to find out about where they've come from. A book like *A Long Way Home* (2014) by Saroo Brierley, plus its 2016 film adaptation, *Lion*, brings these two elements together for audiences, in a recognisable yet subtly different way. By having an Indian man, lost as a child (and adopted by a family in Australia), who must return to Calcutta to discover his heritage, this is a story that is 'the same... but different'. What's stopping writers from looking for other diverse characters who must do something similar?

- **The Stranger.** A stranger, male or female, goes into a community where, initially, s/he is a complete outcast. For various reasons, this character will try to get the community – whether a rural village or a colony of space aliens – to trust him or her. Often they do this with an ulterior motive in mind. However, by the time the community comes around, the stranger has begun to identify with the people there and defects to their side. (*Avatar*, anyone?? Being the most successful film of all time, it's unsurprising this character has made such a splash in the spec pile! Intriguingly, when I ask writers whether they've watched *Avatar*, many will claim they haven't seen it or, if they have, that they dislike it.)

  <u>**HOW TO FLIP IT:**</u> Heavily associated with the White Saviour again, The Stranger is nearly always a white male going into a community of 'natives', though sometimes it will be a white woman. The problem is less the' storyline than the patronising notion that the natives can only win against the antagonistic force with the help of said White Saviour. Flipping it, then, so a person of colour takes this role could be a really interesting starting point in subverting this overdone trope.

It should be noted that none of these characters (or the plotlines they find themselves in) is inherently 'bad'. There has been some really good published and produced content featuring them that has kept audiences entertained, which is what this writing lark is all about. However, if, as new writers and creators, we want to make a big impact, we would be wise to study what has gone before and look to being more diverse with our own characters and storylines. Not because of any political ideology or sense of responsibility, but to create more of a stir (and thus more potential interest in our work).

THE ISSUE WITH DIVERSE VILLAINS

As we know, every story – whatever the medium – needs some kind of antagonist, whether that's an actual person and/or situation (most frequently, both). Drama is conflict: we don't read novels or watch movies or TV about characters who all have wonderful lives and no problems whatsoever! Even in the case of 'feelgood' stories, there will be some sort of issue or struggle a protagonist has to overcome, in the form of an antagonist. As Oscar-winning screenwriter and producer Julian Fellowes (*Gosford Park*, *Downton Abbey*) asserts: 'Characters can be happy for the last three minutes... until then, it's a bumpy road.'

So, in the case of the antagonist, just as with the protagonist, it's important to remember that, ultimately, the 'baddie' is JUST as much a role function as the 'goodie'. As TV producer Gub Neal points out:

Diversity of characterisation only works if we can see a full range of roles being played out. I think, frequently, there is an inherent fear of casting diversely if the roles are contentious or negative. This is reductive (and constrictive). Minority interests only become fully emancipated when everyone has full access to an entire range of characters. Good, bad and ugly... positive type-casting is as patronising as not casting diversely at all. We need the full range; 'the full English'.

IN A NUTSHELL: We need a 'baddie' in the story – and insisting diverse characters are ONLY represented positively is essentially UNdiverse, not to mention patronising. What we need is VARIETY, across all role functions. This means the issue with diverse villains will disappear, ultimately.

TOP FOUR VILLAINS

I totally agree with Gub, but I also understand why audiences become weary when antagonists are always the same kinds of characters – like genres, subgenres and types of story, these 'types' of antagonists become, at best, stale and boring when considering the top four diverse characters:

- **Race.** Antagonists of different races pitted against white protagonists swiftly become problematic, especially when we consider that notion of the 'Highlander Effect' ('There can be only one!'). When the ONLY person of colour in the narrative is the villain, the message could be construed that 'white = good' and 'black = evil'. When we consider stories in which there are numerous BAME characters, we see that many of these feature white protagonists who travel to 'distant lands' in which savage BAME characters create problems for them; or that a white character must educate and/or save them. Veronica Roth, author of the Divergent trilogy, recently came under fire for using the 'dark-skinned aggressor' trope for her 2017 release, *Carve the Mark*. If all this seems oversensitive, consider all the genres, subgenres and types of stories in which white protagonists lead the story... that's right, nearly all of them! So, it may not be that a story is necessarily the issue by itself, but because of cumulative build-up.

  IN A NUTSHELL: Sometimes swapping a BAME antagonist for a white one can work, especially if it's unusual to see a white antagonist in the type of story you're writing. Other times, if a BAME antagonist is crucial to the story, consider ensuring they are not the *only* person of colour in the narrative. Also, think very carefully about how you portray aggressors – it's a good idea not to lift tribal practices wholesale as 'bad' in order to contrast them with 'good, civilised' white culture. Audiences have moved waaaaay past that.

- **Gender.** In real life, we live in a world of men. Male politicians and other figures of authority dominate everywhere in the free world. This is reflected in the output of stories, either consciously or unconsciously, by creators. As a result, the number of female leads is at a premium, especially in movies. Somewhat ironically then – and as already mentioned – there is a certain pressure that female characters be 'good'. This means that while there are a few female protagonists – some of them morally ambiguous – there are even fewer female antagonists. This lack of female 'badness' is counterintuitive, because it leads to flat characterisation and sidelining of female characters generally. Female characters suffer the 'Highlander Effect' just as much as BAME characters – especially in ensembles. When up to 51% of our potential audiences are women, this seems crazy... and that's before we even consider how gender intersects with race. So we end up with female characters needing to be 'good', with BAME characters often being 'bad'... is it any wonder most writers and creators stay away from that potential hornet's nest altogether when it comes to writing antagonists?

IN A NUTSHELL: While female protagonists are making some ground up, there are even fewer female antagonists. Consider what a female villain could bring to your story – and whether she needs to be white.

- **LGBT.** Historically, there has been a strong link between the LGBT community and (supposed) deviancy in stories, so we have seen many gay and trans antagonists in the past, especially in movies and TV. To be bisexual is to be untrustworthy, such as antagonist Catherine Trammell in *Basic Instinct* (1992). In the past 20 years, it would seem being a bisexual female is more acceptable and less indicative of potential 'evil', though bisexual males are still missing from all role functions (outside homosexual erotica or soap opera). Outside of drama and coming-out stories, to be gay or trans – or both – is to be potentially dangerous, especially in the horror and thriller genres. Buffalo Bill, the antagonist of *The Silence of the Lambs* (1988) by Thomas Harris (plus its 1991 Oscar-winning adaptation), is widely considered in the LGBT community to be the epitome of this type of diverse character. It should be noted both Catherine Trammell and Buffalo Bill are iconic characters, who have stood the test of time because they are both written and performed so well. The problem is not that they exist, but that there is such a lack of variety of LGBT antagonists *overall*.

<u>IN A NUTSHELL:</u> If you can, avoid connecting your LGBT antagonist's sexuality or gender identity to the crimes they're committing, or the problems they're creating for your protagonist. It's been overdone and audiences are moving on from this expectation.

- **Disability.** While protagonists who are disabled are frequently dubbed 'inspiring' in drama, disabled antagonists are often bitter, reduced to the sum of their disability in the same way. Conditions that create twisted bodies and disfigured faces are the biggest issue, as if to be considered ugly is to be evil. If we are to include mental health under the banner of disability, we can also include the 'knife-wielding psycho' trope, where psychosis and psychopathy are mixed with abandon by writers and creators, especially in thrillers and horrors. In recent times, as better understanding of mental health issues prevails, we're seeing a switch to protagonists with these challenges instead, especially in novels. Again, it's the notion of disabled characters mainly existing at either end of the characterisation spectrum that's the problem.

<u>IN A NUTSHELL:</u> Consider making your antagonist's disability incidental in the storyworld (as in *Mad Max: Fury Road*), or to his or her evil ways. If you're writing a story in which psychosis and/or psychopathy figure, make sure you know the difference by doing your research and seeing what has gone before in previous works.

SUMMING UP

✓ The best diverse characters don't feel 'try hard', nor are they box-ticking exercises. These characters feel authentic, natural and, most of all, <u>relevant</u>.

✓ There are three tiers to characterisation: main characters, secondary characters and peripheral characters (or whatever you want to call them). In this section, we concentrated on the protagonist and the antagonist.

✓ Writers must avoid stereotypes and stock characters in all characterisation, but especially when it comes to diverse characters. Research is key.

✓ Some diverse characters only need very small changes, then they seem completely different. Others need more diversity in order to seem different from the 'norm'.

✓ Examples of twists on characterisation may be putting a character we don't expect to see in a certain genre, or 'flipping' it so it's the opposite race or gender to what we expect. Alternatively, we may make their diversity incidental to the plot, especially if audiences are used to seeing stories framed around these characters' differences.

✓ Knowing the difference between archetypes and stereotypes can be the difference between creating a brilliant diverse character and a dull, flat one (or even one that is offensive).

✓ Understanding how protagonists and antagonists work in conjunction with plot is paramount. The best diverse characters inform the plot with their decisions and actions.

✓ Role function refers to what the character DOES in the plot and HOW they push it forward. Motivation refers to what characters WANT.

✓ It's never been easier to find out what audiences are bored with, or what people in the industry are looking for or wish was different about characters, thanks to social media.

✓ Studying what has gone before in your chosen genre, subgenre or type of story will enable you to see the kinds of characters used most often.

✓ Audiences are bored of 'typical' characters doing 'typical' things. Taking something familiar and twisting it is a great idea. Creating something completely out of left field isn't, as they won't recognise it or feel it is relevant.

✓ There are certain messages, themes and ideas that modern audiences prefer to see in stories. It will have been different in the past. It's okay to challenge certain ideas, but sometimes you need to challenge your story or characters instead. Make sure you find out how attitudes change and stay up to date.

✓ Knowing who your target audience is and deciding in advance what your own 'deal breakers' are for your story will give you confidence in pushing forward with your story and the diverse characters in it.

SECONDARIES, SIDEKICKS AND SUBORDINATES

'Sometimes when we are generous in small, barely detectable ways it can change someone else's life forever.'

– Margaret Cho

THE CLUE IS IN THE NAME!

In the second part of the book, we discussed the three tiers of characterisation. Protagonists and antagonists tend to push the story forward, which means, unsurprisingly, that stories tend to revolve around them. Any other character will therefore exist within the orbit of these two main characters. In a bid to ensure secondary characters don't take over from these main roles, secondary characters will have:

- Less 'story space' than main characters
- Less depth than main characters
- Less backstory than main characters

The above is not a judgement of any kind on secondary characters at grassroots level. It is a matter of necessity. No reader or viewer can cope with an infinite number of characters. Remember, as explored in the last section of the book, there are normally around five or six important roles in any narrative, book, TV show or movie – but this usually includes the protagonist and antagonist. That means there will be roughly four important secondaries in any story. In many stories, it will be less.

IN A NUTSHELL: Secondary characters will always be underwritten in comparison to the main characters. They have to be. The clue is in the name: SECONDary.

SECONDARY CHARACTERS AND DIVERSITY

Historically, secondary characters tend to be more diverse generally. You're much more likely to find a secondary character who is female, BAME or LGBT. The major exception tends to be disabled characters, because *if* they appear at all, they will often be in the protagonist's role (especially if we're considering so-called 'inspirational' drama). Alternatively, we may find disabled characters in the antagonist's role, especially if we include mental health under the tag of disability with the much-condemned 'knife-wielding-psycho' trope. Otherwise, shockingly, disabled characters may be missing altogether.

Let's return to the list of archetypes we've already touched on in part two of this book. Just as heroes and villains fall under certain archetypes like – obviously – 'Hero' and 'Ruler', it's immediately apparent there are certain archetypes we see in secondary characters a lot, too. In isolation, archetypes like Magician, Sage, Jester, Innocent and Caregiver lend themselves to secondary characters. Whether you're writing a novel or screenplay, drama is conflict, and it's unlikely these five 'lesser' archetypes could sustain a narrative on their own. As the 'story space' awarded to secondary characters is less than for a protagonist or antagonist, at least two of these archetypes would probably need mixing together to create a main character.

With the above in mind, then, it's unsurprising that diverse secondary characters are frequently seen as underwritten, flat or even offensive. In real terms, they literally are LESS written, because they have to be, since they're not the main character. In addition, historically, female, BAME, LGBT and disabled characters are frequently pushed into secondary parts that quickly become overused, so they can seem boring at best and stereotypical at worst. As a result, it can feel like we've got a stack of characters who are:

- Magical people, whether actually supernatural or not (BAME, LGBT)
- Very Wise Sages (BAME, LGBT, disabled)
- Hilarious Jesters (BAME)
- Innocent Damsels (female)
- Caregivers (BAME, female)

Is it any wonder that audiences are bored with this version of 'diversity'?

But what if you mix it up and assign a secondary character an archetypal role we're NOT used to seeing? For instance, in *I, Robot* (2004), a teenage Shia LaBeouf played the secondary character Farber, an obvious 'Jester' character to Will Smith's protagonist, Detective Spooner. Farber spends all his time in the narrative trying to talk trash like a street hoodlum and failing dismally (and amusingly). The playoff between Farber and Spooner not only reverses the usual white-black power play (as Smith's work is wont to do), but also provides the subtext that Farber is just trying to impress the grown-ups, i.e. he's 'a good kid really'. This is underlined when we see Farber at the front of the line of mutinous humans in the resolution, bravely taking on the evil robots. A small part, Farber is nevertheless memorable, so it's unsurprising LaBeouf went on to much bigger things in Hollywood not long after with *Transformers* (2007).

IN A NUTSHELL: Secondary characters – diverse or not – become boring when they occupy the same types of roles we always see them in. Take a look at your archetypes and see if you can mix your secondary characters up.

ENSEMBLES

The obvious exception to the idea of those three tiers of characters (main – secondary – peripheral) is ensemble casts. In an ensemble cast, principal actors and performers are assigned roughly equal amounts of importance and screen time in a dramatic production. This is especially relevant in television, but also some movies (particularly with reference to 'all-star casts') and some novels, especially those with multiple points of view, i.e. of the same event or new storyworld. This means ensemble casts are prevalent in crime fiction, family sagas (such as literary, historical and/or romance) and fantasy in novels.

The word ensemble comes from the French, meaning 'together' (Latin *insimul*, equivalent to *in* + *simul* together).

Some notable ensemble casts in fiction, film and television are listed below.

NOVEL ENSEMBLES

- *Little Women* by Louisa May Alcott
- *The Stand* by Stephen King
- *Game of Thrones* by George R.R. Martin
- *The Girl on the Train* by Paula Hawkins
- *Imajica* by Clive Barker
- *The Hours* by Michael Cunningham
- *The Cider House Rules* by John Irving
- *Pride and Prejudice* by Jane Austen
- *The Shining Girls* by Lauren Beukes
- *Everything I Never Told You* by Celeste Ng

In novels, there's some leeway as regards how many supporting characters a novelist is 'allowed', depending on the type of book you're writing. In heavily plot-based stories like crime fiction, you may find you end up mirroring the screenwriting model of five or six important secondaries – otherwise you may bamboozle your reader with too many potential suspects. In YA fiction, you may focus on the family and a few school friends/love interests, as teens frequently place relationships at the heart of narratives they're interested in. In thrillers and fantasy, you may prefer the route of the 'lone protagonist' up against a shady corporation or evil king. Literary fiction probably has a potentially limitless number of characters, with many fulfilling a symbolic function, reflecting the theme or message of the story.

IN A NUTSHELL: Novels can technically have as many characters as you like, but in the case of the ensemble it's wise to focus on a chosen few (just like in screenwriting), otherwise it can get too confusing.

MOVIE ENSEMBLES

- *The Breakfast Club* (1985)
- *A Fish Called Wanda* (1988)
- *Reservoir Dogs* (1992)
- *Pulp Fiction* (1994)
- *The Ice Storm* (1997)
- *Magnolia* (1999)
- *Ocean's Eleven* (2001)
- *Gosford Park* (2001)
- *Love, Actually* (2003)
- *Crash* (2004)

Note the 'types' of stories above and how the characters usually orbit around a place, event (such as a heist, takeover or weather) or theme (such as relationships). Often ensembles focus on all three of these things. Otherwise, barring ensembles, if a movie seems to have a very large cast, this is usually an illusion; most of the 'extra' characters will in fact be peripheral, rather than those all-important five or six important secondaries.

If it seems like ensembles were particularly popular in the late nineties/early noughties, it's because they were. If something proves popular with audiences, then, generally speaking, more will be provided! Like anything, film tends to follow 'fashion' in this way. More modern ensemble movies include *The Expendables* (2010), *Crazy, Stupid, Love* (2011) and *Marvel's The Avengers* (2012), but ensembles don't seem to have made a massive comeback across the board in movies... yet.

IN A NUTSHELL: Movie ensembles tend to focus on a group of characters doing a specific job (such as a heist or mission), or their reactions to an event or something else that has happened (often traumatic).

TELEVISION ENSEMBLES

- *M*A*S*H* (1972–83)
- *Cheers* (1982–93)
- *The Golden Girls* (1985–93)
- *Friends* (1994–2004)
- *ER* (1994–2009)
- *Cold Feet* (1997–present, after an extended period off-air)
- *The West Wing* (1999–2006)
- *Mistresses* (2008–10)
- *Misfits* (2009–13)
- *Downton Abbey* (2010–15)

Notice how different all the ensembles in this list are in terms of genre, types of story or characters that appear. Whether comedic, political or based around a place, the idea is a GROUP of characters who come together. They may have a 'story of the week' pitted against a 'serial element', as in a returning television series, or they may have to deal with various funny goings-on then reset to zero, as in a sitcom.

While it's true television programmes often have very large supporting casts, it's worth remembering these often grow over a number of seasons. It's no accident *The Simpsons* is named after Springfield's first family; it began with them and they are the primary focus of most episodes, with more and more characters brought in over the last two decades. In contrast, if you were writing a sitcom spec about a dysfunctional family, you would focus almost solely on them – i.e. two adults, plus three children.

IN A NUTSHELL: TV ensembles tend to focus on a group of characters who live in a specific area, or are part of a particular event, time or theme, and sometimes all of the above.

PORTMANTEAUS

The word 'portmanteau' is from the French (as you might expect) and is rooted in *porte* ('carry') and *manteau* ('coat'). A 'portmanteau word' is when you shove two words together to make a new one, such as: spork ('spoon' and 'fork'), labradoodle ('labrador' and 'poodle') and cosplay ('costume' and 'roleplay'). No doubt you know a million more. In the age of social media, it seems more and more portmanteau words are made up every day!

But what has all this got to do with storytelling and diverse characters? A portmanteau story is basically two (or more) stories in one. There are lots of ways to do this, though we're most likely to see this technique in the film world. The most common way is to package up a selection of stories and present them, one after another; these are sometimes known as anthology, package or omnibus movies.

Portmanteaus frequently feature ensemble or large casts of secondary characters, overtly or covertly. As mentioned in the previous section, the larger a cast, the more diverse it usually becomes, so it can be worth considering how diversity fits into your storyworld. The most common ways of presenting portmanteau films are:

- **A theme or idea unites all the stories somehow.** In the case of the London Screenwriters' Festival's *50 Kisses* (2014), 50 microshorts (lasting approximately one or two minutes each) created a narrative in which pretty much anything was possible, but it had to include a kiss. Crowdsourced from a huge number of scripts and films submitted via the Create50 community, the finished film had very different interpretations of that kiss – romance, grief, betrayal – via a melting pot of genres including comedy, action and even horror.

- **An 'outside' element unites all the stories in some way.** In the case of *Creepshow* (1982), a comic book comes alive via animation and we 'see' the stories come to life through the comic-book frame (which then turns to live action). The stories have nothing in common other than being a) 'in' the comic book, and b) a creepy, horror-based story.

- **A character, place in time and/or the storyworld unites the stories somehow.** In the case of the Scottish BAFTA-winning *Night People* (2005), all the characters are confronted with various dilemmas on the same night in Edinburgh. A character from the first part of the film, a taxi driver, picks up another character in the resolution who has had walk-on parts in some of the other stories.

As a genre, horror has a strong history in portmanteau, with classics like J-Horror *Kwaidan* (1964) through to George A. Romero's *Dead Time Stories* (2009) coming under this banner. But in real terms, a portmanteau can be based around any genre, any theme, any collection of characters a writer or filmmaker wants.

Portmanteau movies are very popular with low- and no-budget filmmakers, as they can make a series of short films based on a theme, over an extended period of time, then edit them together. Portmanteau films are about the end result, rather than how it came together, so this can mean many different teams of filmmakers joining forces to crowdsource a movie. This happened with Ridley Scott's *A Life in a Day* (2011), a documentary crowdsourced via YouTube. The London Screenwriters' Festival continues the trend with their second crowdsourced feature, *The Impact*.

That said, there is nothing to stop television from utilising portmanteau storytelling. Its roots are very much in the 'play for today' or 'movie of the week' format, so we are more likely to see one section per week, rather than viewing them altogether. Known as 'anthology series' they are often (though not always) recognisable by the attached names, such as *Walt Disney Presents* (1958–61) or *Nightmares and Dreamscapes: From the Stories of Stephen King* (2006). In the same way, anthologies of short stories are frequently themed and presented in the same way and, again, horror scores highly with readers in this regard, making bestsellers of the likes of *Twisted 50, Volume 1* and *Dark Minds* (both 2016). Writers and filmmakers may all work together in creating such a property, or they may work in isolation, after which a publisher or filmmaker creates a theme or overarching narrative to pull all the strands together.

THE SHORT VERSION: Knowing where you might find an ensemble cast will help you decide how to create and present your own, especially when it comes to diverse characters. Portmanteau stories can help focus your genre, message or storyworld for your potential audience and even help keep costs down, especially if you are an indie filmmaker (or want to work with one!).

PRECINCT DRAMAS

You may find diverse characters where there are large casts of secondaries, especially if it's a precinct drama. A precinct drama is a story in which the storyworld is constant, but the characters may change. Precinct dramas are most often seen on television and may also be called a 'returning drama series' or 'continuing drama' (sometimes a soap opera). Returning drama series like *Death in Paradise*, *Benidorm* or *Holby City* may be called precinct dramas, and also soaps like *EastEnders*, *Coronation Street* or *Home and Away*. The basic idea is that the storyworld is the ONE thing that is non-negotiable. Viewers in effect tune in to see the goings-on in that place via the characters who live or work in it.

In terms of novels, it could be argued some series are precinct dramas – IF the said novels place the storyworld at the heart of the story linking them together, rather than simply using the same protagonist each time. The incredibly popular middle-grade series *Sweet Valley High* did this in the nineties, branching out from original main character twins Elizabeth and Jessica. Eventually the series included the whole high school, so multiple characters got their own books focused on them individually.

A modern example would be YA author Sarah Dessen, who writes a different protagonist each time, but sets all her stories on the Wildflower Ridge estate, so characters from other books may 'cross over' into other novels. I borrowed this idea for my own YA series *The Decision*, setting both books in the fictional seaside town of Winby. Both my protagonists appear in each other's books, though they don't actually meet.

Precinct dramas in terms of movies are rare. Movies tend to focus on franchise potential if they're going for a number of movies, so this usually means the same protagonist or groups of characters appear in each one. That said, occasionally some movie franchises will return with completely new characters, even within the same storyworld timeline. *Dawn of the Planet of the Apes* (2014) focused on completely new human characters, though its protagonist ape Caesar is now an adult, having appeared in the first movie *Rise of the Planet of the Apes* (2011) as a child/adolescent. The same is true of the third in the franchise, *War for the Planet of the Apes* (2017), which again brings forth a new cast of human characters.

IN A NUTSHELL: A precinct drama – no matter the medium – tends to place the storyworld at the heart of the narrative, changing the characters at will (whether groups or individuals). Generally, the bigger the cast of characters, the more diverse it becomes.

THE DUMPING GROUND

The Dumping Ground (2013–present) is a BAFTA award-winning British children's drama series that is broadcast via the CBBC channel. Originally a spinoff from another children's show, *Tracy Beaker Returns* (2010–13), *The Dumping Ground* focuses on a large ensemble cast of children and their care workers who live in a children's home (the aforementioned 'dumping ground'). Storylines in the show have been an eclectic mix, but all have focused on the difficulties children in care face, such as – but not limited to – dealing with abandonment and bereavement; parents with addiction, learning disabilities or mental health problems; or being fostered and/or adopted by new parents.

What's particularly interesting about *The Dumping Ground* is the fact it's predominantly a comedy, yet deals with very real issues children in care face. 'It's actually a very dark show under the lightness of touch, and there are some very dark stories there,' says Phil Gladwin, script editor for the series. 'Never forget, these children have all been abandoned, and most of them spend a good part of their time dealing with the damage from that, and yearning for the parents who abandoned them to return and show them some love.'

Another striking element of *The Dumping Ground* is how diverse the cast of characters is. The children come from an array of backgrounds, not just in terms of gender, race, nationality or socio-economic status, but disability, too: there are characters who are wheelchair users; those with mobility and speech issues caused by cerebral palsy; characters with autism and other learning disabilities; one who is a little person. According to Phil Gladwin:

> The central set-up gives you a group of great characters who are free to behave very badly (which is always great to watch) and yet you forgive them for kicking off because you know they're in pain. The archetypal story for the show is that the DG lets them find a new home. That's a kind of healing very attractive to watch, and very powerful, when it's done well and subtly.

What's brilliant about *The Dumping Ground* is how it goes against 'expected' moral judgements: there are no handy or contrived shortcuts to characterisation based on societal stigmas and prejudice. Parents, young and old, rich and poor, black and white, have failed their kids in some way, meaning they've ended up at the Dumping Ground. Given that so many writers fear 'box ticking' when asked for more diversity, *The Dumping Ground* illustrates that fresh, relatable characters can grow from being intentionally inclusive.

IN A NUTSHELL: Regardless of what you want to write yourself, watch a show like *The Dumping Ground* to see how being intentionally inclusive can feed storylines, without going OTT on diversity as something unique, but incorporating it as part of the 'normal' world.

TROPES ARE TOOLS

At this juncture, it's worth discussing the word 'trope', which you'll have no doubt seen flying all over the interwebz, usually with a negative connotation attached. As far as lay people are concerned, it seems, 'trope = bad writing'. In modern times, especially via social media, the term is synonymous with 'I don't like this' and/or 'cliché'.

But this is where it gets confusing for writers. Tropes are 100% necessary for writing. A trope (in the story sense) is literally any plot, character, setting, device or pattern that we recognise as such. I've already listed a number of tropes in the last couple of sections, but other much-used character tropes that crop up regularly include:

- Wicked Old Miser
- Bad Cop
- Crazy Cat Lady
- Hillbilly
- Dirty Old Man

I don't even need to explain these to you, because you know exactly what they are. These tropes are cemented into our society and culture. You can probably think of at least one character you've seen who makes use of this trope, or maybe even an entire series that uses ALL of them (hint: it's animated and most of the characters are yellow).

Writers NEED tropes because they need a shorthand to introduce characters to the audience. Whether you're writing a novel or screenplay, time is always at a premium – and we have to hit the ground running, story-wise. This means we can't spend ages telling all about the background of the characters BEFORE the story began. Our readers and audiences simply will not allow it.

What's more, no matter what social media says, readers and audiences LIKE the familiarity of tropes. They enjoy the familiarity of recognising certain characters and situations, plus the excitement these bring, especially when our expectations are twisted in interesting ways. So, what readers and audiences hate are not the actual tropes, but the PREDICTABILITY of the 'same-old, same-old', used in samey ways.

Also, don't forget, our readers and audiences have certain expectations. If we're reading a crime novel or watching a thriller movie or TV show, the characters will reflect this. In addition to the obligatory detective or seeker character as the protagonist, as well as the killer as the antagonist, you'll probably need a companion or colleague for each of them. You'll probably need at least one red herring character who is falsely accused, too. All of these are character tropes. (Some of my Bang2writers have told me the word 'trope' seems too toxic now, so I suggest they call them 'conventions' instead.)

THE SHORT VERSION: A story is not good or bad based on whether it has tropes. ALL STORIES HAVE TROPES. A story is good or bad based on how these tropes are used. We like tropes for their familiarity; we hate them when they are predictable, boring or are used too much. Writers need to pinpoint the 'same-old, same-old' tropes in the types of stories and characters they use and either avoid them, or twist them in a new way.

TROPES VERSUS CLICHÉS

So, it's not really tropes that readers and audiences – and writers! – hate, but clichés. The issue is, certain characters are being used too much, in the same ways, in the same types of story. When there aren't enough of those characters in the first place, these endless, samey, clichéd versions of diverse characters can feel like a big UP YOURS to marginalised groups. Lots of people think they know how to fix this and I'd be lying if I said I wasn't one of them. However, let's look first at the suggestions so far.

When it comes to female characters, we have the Bechdel Test. It was suggested by writer Alison Bechdel via her 1985 comic strip, *Dykes to Watch Out For*, that a work of fiction should feature at least two women or girls who talk to each other about something other than a man or boy. The requirement that the two women or girls must be named is sometimes added. This is the most well-known, most-quoted and most-utilised test, with entire film festivals and websites devoted to whether certain works pass it or not. In 2013, Sweden even decided to add a Bechdel rating to all its films on cinema release.

Much discussion surrounds the Bechdel Test, such as:

- **FOR:** It's a great way to get writers to consider how they utilise female characters in their stories, especially new writers or those who have never noticed this issue before.

- **AGAINST:** What does 'about a man' mean? Are we talking romance only, or anything he's doing, in any genre? Does this cover just ONE instance of talking about a man, or do the characters have to ONLY talk about men? Without context, it's meaningless.

- **FOR:** There are too many WAGs generally; we need more diversity in terms of female characters.

- **AGAINST:** A film considered 'feminist' in content may not pass Bechdel; a film that is a feminist's NIGHTMARE may still pass Bechdel. Ack.

- **FOR:** It's a good test to remember when trying to avoid the 'Highlander Effect', especially when it comes to the Girl Character.

- **AGAINST:** If men occupy the two lead roles of protagonist and antagonist most often, of course the female secondaries are talking about him/them.

- **FOR:** The Bechdel Test is so open it can be applied to any medium: fiction, film or TV.

- **AGAINST:** The Bechdel Test was never meant to be authoritative; it is a joke in a comic strip.

As for me, I fall very much in the AGAINST camp in terms of being too slavish as regards Bechdel. If that sounds odd given my predisposition for wanting better female characterisation and female-centric stories, it's because I don't believe the Bechdel Test can provide either of these things. I think it's a handy and valuable starting point, but ultimately that's all it is. Nothing more, nothing less.

IN A NUTSHELL: The Bechdel Test is great if you've never thought about the issues and differences of female characters before. But that's it. Other than that, it has major limitations.

THE BECHDEL TEST AND DIVERSITY

There are other versions of the Bechdel Test for other diverse characters, not just female ones. With reference to race, it's 'two people of colour talking to one another about something other than race/white people', whereas the LGBT community adds that the characters' LGBT status should be neither a source of comedy nor tragedy. The disabled community includes something similar to the LGBT version. Again, the value to new writers, and to the represented groups, of tests like these is obvious – but only as a starting point.

Being too slavish towards certain ideals, and saying certain stories, characters or elements 'shouldn't' be used, just serves to create hellish, albeit well-meaning, hoops for writers to jump through. As an obvious example, some comedy succeeds in being funny simply because it's so near-to-the-knuckle. Also, what about those female, BAME, LGBT or disabled writers, filmmakers and other creators who want to tell stories that are somehow **against** their own version of the Bechdel Test, yet are nevertheless authentic, based on their own real, lived experiences?

In the long term, relying on tests to inform diverse characters and stories simply wouldn't work and might even lead to an impoverishment of ideas as writers become too afraid to create. Readers and audiences would certainly complain about that, too! So, here's my own solution to the issues: forget about tests and theory, or trying to jam your characters and stories into a particular box. That way madness lies. Instead, avoid clichés and work on your characters and make them unusual (though still recognisable) so there is a better variety.

IN A NUTSHELL: Tests such as Bechdel are a great starting point for new ways of thinking, but, in the long term, will NOT deliver better characters and better stories. Instead, avoid cliché and lazy writing by twisting readers' and audiences' expectations. Don't provide the same types of characters in the same types of story as standard.

DISPOSABLE SEX WORKER

If tropes are tools, there will be certain elements we are used to seeing in narratives, whether in fiction, TV or film. What these are can depend on the storyworld and/or genre: for example, we expect to see crimes in crime fiction – that goes without saying. However, where there is crime, there is also a victim and this is very often what has come to be known in critiques as the Disposable Sex Worker.

As we might expect, the Disposable Sex Worker character can most often be found in crime fiction novels, thriller movies (especially gangster) and TV shows involving crime elements, or prison. The overriding belief in society is that women are only sex workers because they have to be (indeed, even the phrase 'sex worker' is under scrutiny, the idea being that these women are automatically exploited and unable to make their own choices in a male-dominated world). So, sex worker characters are nearly always female and, very often, tragic. They will spiral into addiction, abusive relationships, homelessness and/or have their children taken away. Female sex worker characters may be teenagers, but they're not often older than approximately 25. Statistically, we're more likely to see a sex worker who is a trans woman before we see a male sex worker.

This unconscious belief by writers that ALL sex workers are tragic, lost girls pervades most fictional writing in which such women appear. It's extremely difficult to find stories where sex workers are presented as women (and men) in control of their own lives and destinies. Regardless of how a writer personally feels about sex work, even a cursory glance at social media will put writers in touch with real-life sex workers at the touch of a button. Author Ava Marsh wrote *Untouchable*, a 2015 novel that focuses on Grace (aka Stella), a high-class escort who is embroiled in a murder and subsequent government scandal. When I asked Ava how she did her research for *Untouchable*, she answered: 'I read an awful lot of escort blogs. They're a loquacious bunch! Plus I knew a few girls and they gave me the lowdown.'

Ava is right when she says sex workers spend a lot of time online sharing their views and experiences. While you need to Google with care(!), they're easy to find, especially on blogging platforms like Wordpress or social media sites like Twitter. I follow dominatrix @ iamyevgeniya on Twitter, who explains further: 'There are different kinds of sex workers: survival, part-time, full-time, lifers, etc... the survival sex worker stories are the ones that are usually written about and they've become the stand-in for all sex workers.'

If we don't see a sex worker character alive, we may see her dead instead. This trope is known as Disposable Sex Worker and is frequently just a body, not a character at all. She will turn up, lifeless and beautiful, like a doll, naked or semi-clothed, posed or unceremoniously dumped. This trope operates right on the very end of the angel/whore scale, the idea being this character 'gets what she deserves'. Some commentators and audience members argue online that 'too many' female secondary characters work in the sex industry, though they rarely express empathy for the character in the trope, nor do they take issue with the high level of male characters who are pimps, murderers, gangsters or mafiosi in the same types of stories or storyworlds, which I always find intriguing.

Sex workers who are not just bodies or tragic victims are at a premium in modern storytelling. We rarely hear about the realities of sex work, or the problems sex workers have with the law or the societal stigma attached. In fact, when I flag stereotypical sex-worker characters up with writers, they'll often admit to worries about 'glamorising sex work' if their characters are not a complete downer! Yet the answer to this is the same as with ALL characterisation: 'I'd advise any writer that sex workers are people. So, what motivates them? Usually, the same stuff that motivates other people,' says @ iamyevgeniya.

Lastly, there are some obvious pitfalls writers frequently fall into when writing sex-worker characters: 'You have your work persona and your regular persona,' says @iamyevgeniya. 'Many authors and screenwriters simply cover the work persona without realising that it's not everything. It's like assuming a high-school principal is just as stern in their private life as in their public one – it's simply not true.' This is a great point, and one Ava Marsh got right in *Untouchable*: her protagonist Grace's work persona is known as Stella and behaves significantly differently to her 'true' self in the course of the plot. This notion of having 'two faces' is hugely interesting for any writer, which is why it's puzzling writers do not do it more... until you figure out most simply haven't done their research. They've taken everything they know from stereotypes and stock characters. Ooops!

IN A NUTSHELL: Writers wanting to create a sex-worker character different to the tragic 'norm' would do well to actually consult with sex workers! This is easier than ever, thanks to the internet. Some sex workers even offer consultation services for writers, like @ iamyevgeniya. She's not cheap – she starts at $100 an hour. But given that diverse sex-worker characters are SO unusual, if you can come up with a great one who's both authentic and relatable, it could be money well spent.

OTHER HOTLY DEBATED TROPES

Thanks to the internet, certain tags have been assigned to these role functions we see a lot in stories, especially when it comes to marginalised characters. Some, like 'Mary Sue' (mentioned in part two of this book), exist solely on the internet; others have become more widespread because of it, especially when it comes to blogs and social media. Others take their inspiration from society itself and get reflected in stories. Here are the tropes you may see most often in the discussion on diverse secondaries:

- **Manic Pixie Dream Girl (aka MPDG).** Usually very beautiful, usually white, this is a woman with infinite wisdom whose position in the narrative is to show the male protagonist where he's going wrong in his life. MPDGs don't tend to show up in fiction and seem to be pretty rare in TV as well, but turn up in movies A LOT. Film critic Nathan Rubin coined the term after observing Kirsten Dunst's character in *Elizabethtown* (2005), stating that MPDGs are 'that bubbly, shallow, cinematic creature that exists solely in the fevered imaginations of sensitive writer-directors to teach broodingly soulful young men to embrace life and its infinite mysteries and adventures'. This prompted a huge wave of discussion online as to whether MPDGs were 'good' characterisation or not, plus the lens was seemingly applied with abandon to every secondary female character in movies outside horror at one point. Rubin has since disowned the term, but you'll still find people talking about it. It's generally thought MPDGs are automatically bad characterisation, though I'd argue the toss (quelle surprise!) and say some GREAT characters are MPDGs: Clementine in *Eternal Sunshine of the Spotless Mind* (2004) and Summer in *(500) Days of Summer* (2009) to name just two.

HOW TO FLIP IT: What about a Manic Pixie Dream Boy, like Jesse in *Pitch Perfect* (2012)? Also, it's worth considering, when it comes to genre, that the issue is largely with ubiquity when it comes to the MPDG. She feels stale and boring in the romance stakes, but if you put her in another genre, she could feel fresh. Melody in gangster movie *Don Hemingway* (2013) is arguably a MPDG and she works.

- **Crying WAG (aka 'Reactress').** Wives and girlfriends – or WAGs – tend to be the default position of female actresses, which is unsurprising when we consider so many movies have straight male protagonists. In movies like *Everest* (2015), *Foxcatcher* (2014) or *American Sniper* (2014), it would seem the female characters of the story exist solely to react (hence the 'reactress' tag) to what's happening to their men by crying down the phone. Ack. The WAG role function is despised so much by so many female audience members that many great roles in this category get ignored or forgotten, such as Bianca in *Creed* (2015), which is a fantastic, three-dimensional role, every bit as much as Adrian's was in the original *Rocky* movies. Intriguingly, in the world of TV many female leads are WAGs; in domestic noir novels, too. Yet this doesn't seem to be as much of a problem for certain members of the audience, which I always find intriguing.

HOW TO FLIP IT: It might be obvious, but that's because it is: involve your WAG properly in your protagonist's life! Don't just have her at the end of the phone, or shouting at him for (inevitably) screwing stuff up. If you're going to use the wife or girlfriend trope, make it holistic, Alternatively, why not have a MALE character performing this expected role, either because your male protagonist is gay or bisexual, or because you have a female lead instead?

- **Mammy (aka 'Mammie').** This is a trope relating to the Southern United States for a black woman who works as a nanny and/or general housekeeper, often for a white family. There are some historical links to plantations and/or wet nursing. Examples of the

Mammy trope include 'Mammy Two Shoes', who you may remember as hands, stocking and feet in the old *Tom and Jerry* cartoons; more recent examples would be Minny Jackson and Aibileen Clark in the 2009 novel *The Help*, plus its movie adaptation in 2011.

HOW TO FLIP IT: This is an easy one: why not a white nanny who works for a black family, for once? Or maybe a male nanny (aka 'manny')? Also, since Mammies are noted for their maternal nature, a Mammie of any race who is intellectual, or even a cold fish (who nevertheless looks after the children well), would be strikingly different to the 'usual'.

- **Angry Black Lady (aka 'Sassy Black Woman').** This one is exactly what it says on the tin: an angry black woman will derail the story and/or the characters' worldviews for some reason, often just because she can. She may do this in a witty or funny way (hence the 'sassy' addition) or she may be scary, especially when dealing with white characters. This is a trope that extends from the page – screenplay or novel – all the way into society. Real-life black women will frequently be characterised as bossy, belligerent or unreasonable as standard, even when they have perfectly understandable grievances. Don't believe me? Check out how the media characterise celebrities like Nicky Minaj in comparison to, say, Taylor Swift.

  HOW TO FLIP IT: Believe it or not, even a trope as tired and potentially offensive as this one can be flipped. Despite being white in the comics, Leslie Uggams plays Blind Al in *Deadpool* (2016), a blind, snarky old woman who can match the 'Merc with the mouth' every step of the way ('I miss cocaine!!'). She also performs a mentor/confidante function to Deadpool, of sorts. So, in other words, make sure your black female secondaries have DEPTH, rather than avoiding them altogether.

- **Dragon Lady.** This is essentially the Chinese or East Asian version of 'Angry Black Lady', especially when it comes to aggression.

Like many East Asian-based tropes, she is mysterious, mystical and probably untrustworthy. She seems to appear most in anime, comic books and video games, though recently there was a furore regarding Marvel's *Doctor Strange* (2016), with the casting of Tilda Swinton as The Ancient One. The decision to cast a white woman instead of an East Asian man or woman was criticised widely, though the filmmakers said they wanted a good female role, but were afraid of inadvertently writing the Dragon Lady trope too broadly. Yet this didn't seem to be a concern for the writers of *Deadpool* as far as Blind Al was concerned, as mentioned in the previous section!

HOW TO FLIP IT: East Asian female characters are frequently magical in some way, like so many BAME characters who appear with white leads; what's more, East Asian women are frequently uber-loud with it. But Lilly in *Pitch Perfect* (2012) is known not only for being ridiculously quiet, but kooky with it.

- **Exotic Eastern Blossom (aka 'Lotus Flower', 'Ornamental Oriental' or 'Flower Vase').** Perhaps harking back to romantic notions of geishas and sexy slave girls(!), secondary female characters will frequently inhabit this role function, especially if they are of Japanese or Chinese descent, and exist in all mediums. This will usually be a servile position to a white male protagonist, who may make her his confidante, or try to rescue her, or both. Whatever the case, she is often highly sexualised and there to be used (hence the 'vase' tag, especially on Twitter). Mako Mori, in giant monsters versus giant robots epic *Pacific Rim* (2013), is notable for NOT filling this role function. Instead she is a holistic character with her own history and problems, plus her connection to white male protagonist Raleigh via The Drift is hinted at as being spiritual, rather than sexual.

HOW TO FLIP IT: Give your East Asian female characters their own problems and ways of looking at the world. Don't make them a vessel for your protagonist to use.

- **Kick-ass East Asian.** The 'kick-ass' part of the name obviously relates to this character's martial arts skills! These characters can be found predominantly in this subgenre of movies, though kung fu, Shotokan karate and tae kwon do sequences, which are popular in Hollywood just now, have become popular with Western audiences. If this guy is on his own, and quiet and unpredictable to boot, then he's probably part of a group that includes characters such as Yin Yang in *The Expendables*, or Hanzo in *Predators* (both 2010). Sometimes KEA is a woman, like Lady Deathstrike in *X2: X-Men United* (2003) or Mai in *Live Free or Die Hard* (2007). If there are multiple Kick-ass East Asians, these will usually be peripheral characters who orbit a 'Mr Big'-type antagonist character, like Mr Jang in *Lucy* (2014).

  HOW TO FLIP IT: What if your Kick-ass East Asian character could fight, but also performed another function – i.e. comic relief? KEA is always so serious all of the time and there's no reason s/he should be. Alternatively, why not have a more nuanced Kick-ass East Asian character, such as Danny in *Unleashed* (2005)?

- **Nerdy Asian.** Most likely male, these characters may be of Pakistani, Indian, Chinese, Japanese or Korean descent (to name just a few). Unlike white geek characters (who are likely to be geniuses with computers), pure maths is likely to be this character's speciality. If this character is in school, he is also likely to be extremely quiet and probably bullied by white characters (especially into doing jocks' homework for them). In the adult world, this character will be an accountant or similar. Whatever the case, Nerdy Asian is never a sexual character and East Asian men in particular are hardly ever seen kissing – well, anyone! Straight or gay, this character seems completely asexual most of the time.

  HOW TO FLIP IT: Shows of strength or physical prowess (beyond martial arts) are at a premium for this secondary character. Yet Minho in *The Maze Runner* (both the 2009 novel and its movie adaptation in 2014) is extremely smart and extremely physical, without a karate kick in sight. Jin in *Lost* (2004–10) is a fully realised male East Asian character, who is also a sexual being.

- **Magical Negro.** This term was coined by film director Spike Lee and describes when a black character is in a servile position, usually in the storyline of a white protagonist. He is usually male but attributed wise, almost magical, powers (even outside the supernatural world). Magical Negros exist in all mediums, but especially novels and film. Particular points of contention include *The Green Mile* (1996) by Stephen King, plus its movie adaptation in 1999; also the movie *The Legend of Bagger Vance* (2000). Some writers and creators – both black and white, by the way – fail to see the issue here, believing it's a complimentary role. Others point out that, especially in the case of movies and TV, secondary characters who are magical are more frequently cast as Asian or Black, so it's more to do with the actual mechanics of filmmaking. The impact of casting can be massively underestimated and will be explored later in this section of the book. Overall, however, even supposedly complimentary roles can serve to 'other' BAME characters, so I'd always support more variety, especially when the 'same-old, same-old' gets so dull. As author Paula Daly points out, 'I'm tired of reading about and watching black characters who are totally virtuous and selfless. I'd like to see more conflict in these characters.' Drama IS conflict, after all!

  HOW TO FLIP IT: What if your BAME secondary characters are as clueless about what's going on as your protagonist? In the case of Renee in the post-apocalyptic novel *The Fireman* (2016) by Joe Hill, she literally has none of the answers for protagonist Harper. However, this doesn't stop her being a brilliant, powerful and three-dimensional character, with no 'magical' qualities (and neither is she an 'angry' or 'sassy' black lady).

- **Sacrificial Minority (aka 'Expendable Hero').** Originally the 'sacrificial minority' was loosely translated as 'the black guy dies first', especially in the horror genre, a cliché that is mercilessly made fun of in the *Scream* (1996) franchise. However, in recent times – especially the last 30 or 40 years – this idea seems to have evolved to the notion of the 'Expendable Hero', a secondary character who dies so the rest of the group – not to mention the protagonist – can live. These characters are frequently BAME and usually male. In addition, white male secondary characters will also do this and it's a role the audience usually cherishes and invests in heavily, hence the choruses of 'Noooooooooooo!' when this character dies. The Bible passage 'Greater love hath no man than this... that he lay down his life for his friends' has particular resonance here. Again, BAME actors will most often be cast in secondary positions, so many argue it's actually more to do with the mechanics of filmmaking than writing. Whatever the case, if you've ever met an actor – BAME or not – many subscribe to the notion, 'If I can't be the protagonist, I want to die SPECTACULARLY!!'

HOW TO FLIP IT: What about a female Expendable Hero? They do exist, though there aren't many. In movies, there's Betty in *Resident Evil: Extinction* (2007), and Mags Flanaghan in *The Hunger Games: Catching Fire* (2013) also comes to mind.

- **Dead Lesbian (aka 'Bury Your Gays').** This is an argument waiting to happen that erupts on the internet with regularity, especially when a much-loved gay character dies in a TV show. Gaining prominence around the time Willow's girlfriend, Tara, died in *Buffy the Vampire Slayer* (1997–2003), this controversy seemed to hit new heights in 2016 when Lexa, the Grounder Commander in The CW's *The 100* died. Lexa was a powerful and three-dimensional character – who just happened to be gay – and had been celebrated by both the LGBT and straight community alike. Her 'will they, won't they' story with bisexual protagonist Clarke on the show was both groundbreaking and complex, especially considering Lexa also performed an antagonist role function as well as a love interest. This trope is called 'Bury Your Gays' because the LGBT community is frustrated that queerness is often linked to death for characters historically, no matter the medium, but especially on TV. However, some writers and creators argue it's more about the fact *most* LGBT characters are secondary characters, so if there were more LGBT protagonists, there would be fewer gay characters dying (since protagonists die least in stories).

HOW TO FLIP IT: Does your gay secondary character *need* to die? What if there was more than one in your story? Ruth Ware's bestselling novel *In a Dark, Dark Wood* (2015) is notable for having not one but two gay secondary characters, even in a small group of friends. Because... why not?! It also means the reader is unable to attach automatic labels like 'the gay one dies first'!

- **Gay Mentor (aka 'Magical Queer').** Similar to the 'Magical Negro' trope, this is a gay secondary character who will have all the answers for our (straight) protagonist, especially when it comes to issues of the heart. The general idea is that a gay character – usually a man – understands the world, due to growing up persecuted for his sexuality. He will counsel the protagonist to take a leap of faith on this basis. This character crops up over and over in romantic comedies, novels, TV and movies but, intriguingly, doesn't seem to attract the same level of vitriol online as the Magical Negro. Two gay mentors of note who are three-dimensional and interesting/funny are George in *My Best Friend's Wedding* (1997) and Jack in the romance novels series *Another Cup of Coffee* by Jenny Kane.

HOW TO FLIP IT: What if your gay secondary character was as unlucky in love as your protagonist? Or what if your gay mentor wasn't a white male for once?

- **Tragic Trans (aka 'Sad Trans').** Once cast staunchly under the 'deviant homosexual' umbrella in such movies as *The Crying Game* (1992) and *Ace Ventura: Pet Detective* (1994) – if they appeared at all. Typical representations of trans characters in fiction, film and television have changed radically in recent times, especially the last five years. Now the dominant narrative pertaining to being trans is to be considered 'tragic', with death and suicide closely associated with trans characters. While not inauthentic – trans people are more likely to be murdered, or commit suicide – it is obviously wearying for the LGBT community to 'always' be portrayed in this way. Jared Leto's Oscar-winning performance as Rayon in *Dallas Buyers' Club* (2013) is largely credited with turning the spotlight on trans characters, though trans activists are often highly disparaging of the character, saying she is unrealistic and even 'trans-misogynistic'.

HOW TO FLIP IT: What if your story involved a transgender person, but wasn't specifically about being trans (or suicide/death), for once? As hated as *The Crying Game* is within the trans community for *that* scene, Dil is nevertheless a character who just so happens to be trans. Similarly, in TV shows like *Orange Is the New Black*, characters like Sophia may face prejudice for being trans, but that is not the sole element of her storylines. In novels, *He's Gone* by Alex Clare (2016) features DI Robyn Bailley, a police detective who is a trans woman.

TROPES IN A NUTSHELL: These tags may get thrown around on the internet, or assigned to fiction, film and TV with abandon. But just because such a tag exists doesn't mean your character is 'bad'. Nor does your use of such a trope mean an automatic 'fail'. Remember, tropes are tools. We're not reinventing the wheel here and we have to start somewhere. That said, don't repeat stuff we've seen a gazillion times before, either – at the very least, it's stale and boring.

SUPPORTING CHARACTERS

Writers, filmmakers and other creators may understand the role functions and motivations of protagonists instinctively enough to write them well by accident, rather than design. Most writers know their protagonist needs or wants something for some reason, plus their antagonist wants to stop that protagonist from getting it for their own reasons (or vice versa, especially in the case of the thriller or some dramas, particularly those with passive protagonists). At base level, we're talking about WHY the protagonist is doing what s/he is doing and WHY the antagonist is trying to ensure the opposite. These two things work together; their character motivations and character role functions are complementary.

So, it will be at the second level, within the supporting cast, that characterisation will frequently start to go wrong. In short, writers will not know:

- How many supporting characters they should have
- What character differentiation means
- Why they need supporting characters

IN A NUTSHELL: If writers don't know WHY they need secondary characters, their unpublished novels and spec screenplays may become bogged down with too many characters, their characters may all sound the same, or they may have no specific function in the plot. Perhaps all of the above!

CHARACTERISATION 101

The two things every writer must know, regardless of medium, are character motivation and the character role function of EVERY character, main or secondary. These are non-negotiable! So, even at secondary level, when it comes to characterisation, we're talking:

WHO IS DOING WHAT AND WHY?

Remember, character motivation is what a character WANTS; character role function is what a character DOES in terms of pushing the story forward. But this element frequently gets forgotten when it comes to secondary characters. Every secondary needs their own 'want', however small. After all, they don't know the story isn't about them! Similarly, the secondary character should HELP or HINDER the main characters in their respective missions or goals. I often ask my clients to draw up lists of whether their secondaries are 'Team Protag' or 'Team Antag', plus why. While crude, this can help a writer focus on which secondaries are useful and which are surplus to requirements.

Writers, by the way, will often fall in love with specific characters 'just because' and this is never more obvious than with diverse characters. Often, a writer will pick a bog-standard protagonist we've seen umpteen times before, yet pour their heart into the secondaries. But why not have a diverse protagonist and/or antagonist instead? Don't be afraid to break the mould (as long as you don't go OTT!).

IN A NUTSHELL: Secondary characters need their own motivations in order to feel three-dimensional, plus they need a reason to be in the story in the first place. They exist to help or hinder the protagonist or antagonist.

A REASON TO LIVE

Supporting characters begin to feel two-dimensional when they don't have a reason to exist in the plot (either HELPING or HINDERING the two main characters in their respective goals); or they may feel like cardboard cut-outs when their own beliefs, thoughts, feelings and position in the story are not sufficiently included. Instead, secondary characters become decoration, or expositional crutches, there solely to dole out information to the protagonist and antagonist (and therefore the reader). To combat this, we have to address the questions asked above:

- **How many supporting characters should there be?** In screenplays, whether short, feature-length or TV pilot, there are usually in the region of five or six important supporting characters (if we're assuming there are a protagonist and antagonist as well, making eight total). In produced content, there are frequently much fewer than this in modern films and TV, very often between just two and four supporting characters.

IN A NUTSHELL: Once you have your protagonist and antagonist, there are always FEWER important secondary characters to write than you think, anything between two and six usually. In a novel you may have more, but screenwriting craft can help you with this, too (and may be advisable, to keep you 'focused').

- **What does character differentiation mean?** Writers hear about characters needing differentiation and immediately think they need to ensure they're all different on the SURFACE LEVEL. This means they have characters talking differently, or characters of different genders, races or similar, as if this will somehow magically mean their characterisation has depth across the board. However, differentiated characters does not refer to this, but rather the role function each one has in advancing the plot. If your protagonist and antagonist each want something, then each of your important secondaries has to pull his/her weight in helping your protagonist or antagonist obtain his or her goal (or not). It's that simple.

IN A NUTSHELL: You cannot make your characters diverse randomly. Each of your secondary characters needs a DIFFERENT ROLE in helping or hindering your protagonist or antagonist and pushing the story forward, otherwise they are not pulling their weight in the plot, so need to be cut or merged.

- **Why do stories need supporting characters?** This is where your research comes in again. If you know who your target audience is, what they're expecting and why, plus how you can twist those expectations, you can make insightful choices in your characterisation. Certain role functions and archetypes go with certain genres and subgenres and are 'no-brainers' – it would be difficult, for example, to write an action-adventure with no hero to save the day (though not impossible). So it's probably a good idea to include one, plus his/her 'expected' helpers like the Mentor or Comic Relief. Sitcoms frequently revolve around dysfunctional families, whether literal blood relatives or those brought together by jobs or living conditions (such as flat shares). This doesn't mean they 'have' to be these things, though. If you can transplant that 'dysfunctional family' into a storyworld we don't expect – for example, space, like *Red Dwarf* (1988) – then your sitcom could stand out.

It's also worth remembering there are new ways of looking at genres and subtypes all the time. It once would have been thought a detective, professional or amateur, was 100% necessary for crime fiction, yet now we have domestic noir, plunging a lone protagonist into a detective-style position. In this case, many of your secondary characters will be hostile to this protagonist and she may have few, if any, friends or confidantes. It would, however, be absolutely impossible to write crime fiction without a crime. A 'deal breaker', in fact!

IN A NUTSHELL: Knowing WHY protagonists and antagonists need supporting characters (plus what 'side' your supporting cast are 'on') really helps in choosing your secondary characters and may even help you break new ground, especially when it comes to diversity.

CASTING CONTRARINESS

As mentioned, secondary characters are more likely to be diverse, so this has the knock-on effect that diverse characters are historically more likely to be 'underwritten' in comparison with non-diverse characters. So the obvious thing to do: write more non-diverse protagonists and antagonists! Great, sorted.

But wait! There are obviously issues with this approach, too – not least because we still need diverse secondary characters as well. When thinking about diverse characterisation across the board, writers will often find variations of the following four debates, both for and against:

- **We don't always want to read or watch 'who' we are.** In novels, the average reader is a woman. But that doesn't mean women don't like to read about male protagonists, or storyworlds in which men, or groups of men, are the main characters. With movies, too, women like to watch male heroes as well as female ones. Similarly, though most people are not LGBT, there are still lots of stories across all mediums about this group! For example, apparently, more straight women read homosexual erotica than gay men! The opposite is true of stories featuring disabled people: they do not appear very much in stories – in any medium – yet it's estimated nearly 20% of the UK and US populations have a disability.

- **Diversity and democracy are often (wrongly) conflated.** When the majority in an audience belongs to a certain demographic, generally speaking, this is reflected in characterisation. This is particularly obvious with movies and race: in the UK and US, *most* people are white, so it might be argued this is why there are more white characters overall. But most people are not LGBT, yet there are lots of stories about them; and many people are disabled, yet there are VERY FEW stories about them. In TV and novels, women are the primary consumers, so we see a lot of stories featuring them as characters in these mediums... yet we don't see this translate to film. Weird, considering females are 51% of the potential audience.

- **Intentional inclusion is secondary on most people's enjoyment radar.** While it's true some readers and viewers go out of their way to be inclusive in their consumption of novels, films and TV, most of us don't. We're interested, first and foremost, in whether the story seems interesting and whether we will enjoy it. When time is at a premium, we want to enjoy ourselves in our leisure time, so it's very unlikely we will bother with books, movies or TV shows that sound boring or irrelevant to us.

- **Lack of diversity ON PURPOSE.** In some storyworlds, a single gender has to dominate – for example, in single-sex environments, like prisons or some boarding schools. It would not make sense in terms of the storyworld to have gender parity here. The same goes for certain storyworlds involving race, especially when it comes to issues of class and socio-economics, but also rural areas, which are typically more white-centric in the Western world. It's also worth remembering that sometimes certain themes/stories do not lend themselves to diversity. While *Mad Max: Fury Road* included disability in its storyworld, it was ultimately a story about white supremacy, so it makes sense the War Boys were effectively all pale in the vein of a Nazi-like Aryan 'master race'.

IN A NUTSHELL: Being for or against diversity in a single story doesn't automatically make that publisher, producer, agent or filmmaker an arsehole. When sales are paramount and there are certain 'deal breakers' for audiences, going against the tide for the sake of it can be a futile endeavour. Sometimes thinking AROUND potential constraints or casting issues can get you further.

CASTING ISSUES

Because diverse characters are not 'the norm' in storytelling, any potentially diverse character becomes 'extraordinary', or at least super-noticeable in a story. This means any diverse character – especially secondary characters with lesser story space – can easily become a vehicle for stereotypes or offensive tropes and ideas, intentional or not. This is especially clear in film and television where actors must be employed to render the characters as image. But authors are not off the hook either. Bestselling and/or critically acclaimed novels will usually be adapted for the screen, plus movements like 'We Need Diverse Books' mean potential readers are becoming more and more demanding about diverse characters in books generally.

In recent years, the most obvious casting furores online and in the real world have involved race, especially regarding 'whitewashing'. This is the casting of characters who were BAME in the source material as white characters when adapting the story for the screen. This is something industry professionals – particularly white ones – are quick to defend, pointing out the lack of BAME stars to fill this void. These white pros – producers, directors, screenwriters – may profess a desire to cast more BAME people in protagonist roles, but say their hands are tied. They may then say, if audiences want to see more black stars, they need to vote with their wallets and get behind movies with BAME actors and filmmakers at the helm. They may then point to stars such as Michael B. Jordan and filmmakers like Ryan Coogler, whose *Fruitvale Station* (2013) led both to a turn in the *Rocky* franchise with the Oscar-nominated *Creed* in 2015.

While there is truth in all this, it ignores the elephant in the room: the fact that black stars and filmmakers simply get overlooked as standard, from the bottom up. I spoke to actor Daniel Yorke about being a diverse actor and the challenges he and his colleagues face in a predominantly white industry. Also, with spaces for BAME actors at such a premium, some find themselves at an even bigger disadvantage than others: 'Black is semi-marketable; East Asian? Forget it.'

Daniel is a writer, actor and playwright, whose heritage is Singapore Chinese. As well as being vociferous about BAME people's inclusion in the arts, Daniel is an accomplished theatre performer, having appeared with the Royal Shakespeare Company and at the Royal Court, though he is best known for parts in movies such as *The Beach* (2000) and *Rogue Trader* (1999). B2W advocates that writers can learn a lot about characterisation from actors and Daniel speaks eloquently about what secondary characters are for, in terms of pushing the story forward: 'If we're talking about a character like "Jealous Husband", then he needs to oppress his wife; but a character like "Chinese Man" – his dramatic function is to BE Chinese!'

Daniel makes a great point here. Of course a character should not be reduced like this – but they so often are, in books as well as films and TV dramas. Often, race is assumed by the writer, so 'white = default' and BAME characters are noted FOR their 'difference'. On this basis, some people believe BAME actors should 'just stop' taking parts like this, but Daniel disagrees. 'You're in this double bind: in order to work, you have to be *seen* working. You have to take the (stereotypical) roles… but then this traps you as an actor.'

This also chimes with Bethany Black's experience. A comedienne and actor, Bethany is also transgender. She is best known for her stand-up, but also her appearance in Russell T. Davies's Channel 4 comedy shows *Cucumber* and *Banana* in 2015. She argues that getting work boils down to, 'Have they heard of you LATELY?' In other words, getting cast as an actor is like getting writing gigs! In an industry based on referrals, you need to ensure you're at the forefront of everyone's mind (especially when someone asks for that 'casting wish list' former sales agent Samantha Horley references in part two of this book).

IN A NUTSHELL: The industry is white-centric and a reflection of the society we live in. There are all kinds of 'reasons' – both good and bad – why marginalised actors find themselves at the bottom of the pile, but a writer working on spec needn't worry about any of this. If you write an authentic, relevant, diverse lead character who captures the imagination and could potentially make money, all these worries miraculously fly out of the window as publishers and production companies compete for the rights to it!

CASTING CATCH-22S

Other current discussions surrounding casting and diversity involve the notions of 'transface' and 'cripface'. This describes the notion of non-transgender and non-disabled actors playing characters some advocates believe should be played by actors who are trans or disabled in real life. This happens so often that trans people in particular may find themselves consistently played by people who are not transgender. As Bethany Black points out, 'The first time I saw anyone *like* me, on British TV... was me!'

As dramas about disability are favourite Oscar contenders, plus transgender stories have had a significant rise in the past five years, this debate doesn't seem to be going away any time soon. Here's a brief, simplified breakdown of the arguments most commonly seen in articles and on social media:

- **FOR:** We need to see more transgender and disabled actors on-screen, full stop. They need more chances than they are currently being given.

- **AGAINST:** We need the best actors for the individual part. Should we cast a terrible (diverse) actor just because their trans or disabled status is 'right'?

- **FOR:** People need to see that being a wheelchair user, or living with a mental health or learning disability, is not 'the end' of one's creative aspirations.

- **AGAINST:** It isn't always appropriate to cast people with certain disabilities due to health and safety requirements; low-budget films may have limited resources and/or some learning disabilities or mental health issues might mean film sets are too stressful for certain people.

- **FOR:** There can be a happy medium, using disabled actors AND stars. In *Snow White and the Huntsman* (2012), well-known actors such as Ray Winstone and Nick Frost played The Dwarves, but their faces were superimposed on two body doubles, who were little people.

- **AGAINST:** In the case of some stories (like those involving a character having a terrible accident, or degenerative disease), sometimes an able-bodied actor is appropriate casting because part of the story involves him/her being able-bodied first.

- **FOR:** Transgender stars like Laverne Cox (*Orange Is the New Black*) and disabled actors like Robert David Hall (*CSI: Las Vegas*) bring an understanding and authenticity to their roles a non-trans or non-disabled actor simply cannot emulate.

- **AGAINST:** Acting is always a game of pretend; even if actors are playing characters 'like' them, it is fiction, not autobiography.

- **FOR:** We don't tolerate actors 'blacking up' or in 'yellowface', so why should we tolerate non-trans and non-disabled actors playing these characters?

- **AGAINST:** There are hundreds of thousands of black or Asian actors, so to actively exclude them from playing their own race is wrong; in comparison, there is a much smaller pool of disabled actors, and a tiny number of trans actors, so even when actively trying to include them, it can't always happen.

There are obviously lots more, but these are the ones I recorded most often when conducting interviews, or reading articles and threads during the course of my research for this book. I'm not sure this one can ever be resolved adequately. Marginalised actors must get the same opportunities as everyone else, but that last point about there being a very small pool of disabled and trans talent is probably key. But, of course, it's not as simple as that!

'It's a Catch-22 situation,' Bethany agrees. 'There simply aren't ENOUGH diverse actors to play the diverse roles, but whether that is because of lack of opportunity, lack of experience, who knows.' Apparently, for *Cucumber* there was an open casting call and just about every notable trans actor auditioned for Bethany's part. The makers were so stressed about finding the right actor, Bethany tells me Russell T. Davies was going to rewrite the entire episode if Bethany's audition hadn't worked out. Luckily, it did.

IN A NUTSHELL: A lot of attention is being given to this issue and what is 'best' regarding the casting of both disabled and transgender actors (or not). Though lots of armchair critics dish out condemnations, anyone who's actually produced something soon discovers there are multiple non-creative issues that may get in the way of casting disabled and transgender actors.

SUMMING UP

✓ Secondary characters will always play second fiddle to protagonists and antagonists. The clue is in the name! That said, secondary characters must still feel real, fresh and relevant.

✓ Like protagonists and antagonists, secondary characters all have character motivations, but they also have role functions in pushing the story forward. If they don't, they need to be cut or merged with another character.

✓ Ultimately, secondary characters exist to HELP or HINDER the protagonist and/or antagonist in their main goal or mission – but crucially, no secondary character should know s/he is 'just' a secondary.

✓ Somewhere in the region of five or six important secondaries are usually tolerated by readers and audiences, across all mediums. In real terms, however, there are frequently far less.

✓ Ensembles, portmanteaus, precinct dramas and anthologies can present an opportunity for a writer to concentrate on a large collection of diverse characters, because the theme, storyworld and/or setting will serve as the 'starting point' for the story.

✓ Ensembles, portmanteaus and anthologies may mean more characters, which means more potential for diversity – but writers need to know how many is 'too many'.

✓ The Bechdel Test and its variations are a good starting point for those who have never thought about diverse characterisation before, but it has many limitations and shouldn't be used as a 'box-ticking' exercise.

✓ Secondary characters may be more diverse as standard, but that doesn't let writers off the hook. There are lots of samey and boring ways secondary characters are presented, especially in the top four. Also, because of sheer numbers, there are lots of potential pitfalls for secondary characters, which is particularly relevant with regard to stereotypes and stock characters.

✓ Tropes are tools and necessary for writing. When readers and audiences say they dislike tropes, they mean they hate clichés and stereotypes.

✓ Don't try to reinvent the wheel. Often, a small twist to a character is more effective than a complete overhaul. But, to do this, you must know what has gone before in terms of characterisation in your genre, type of story or medium – do your research.

✓ Avoid the 'Highlander Effect' – the notion that there is only ONE diverse secondary character in your storyworld. This has been done to death, in all stories, of all genres, in all mediums. Time for a change.

✓ Character differentiation via diversity is more than just the way a character speaks or looks. A secondary character is instrumental in pushing the story forward every bit as much as a protagonist or antagonist; s/he is not decoration. A random diverse character is no use to the story or to diversity in general.

✓ Knowing what readers and audiences are talking about online regarding tropes can be helpful, as it can stop writers from walking into potential problems further down the line... that said, not all perceptions of characterisation are equal or useful, nor should writers feel paralysed by the potential audience's disapproval.

✓ There will always be casting Catch-22s with your TV show or movie, or if your novel is adapted for the screen. Some readers will also make various demands of your characters' diversity. You have to get that far first, so my advice is: live with it!

✓ Being authentic and relevant when it comes to diverse characterisation always means doing your research as a writer. Know what has gone before when it comes to secondary characters – what has worked well; what has not; plus what has changed and why. Do your due diligence.

✓ Know WHO is doing WHAT and WHY with your diverse secondaries, just as you would any character.

PERIPHERAL POINTERS

'As a writer, you should not judge; you should understand.'

– Ernest Hemingway

WHAT IS A PERIPHERAL CHARACTER?

Peripheral characters are those characters present in a novel or screenplay who do not perform a specific character function in pushing the story forward. Instead, when peripheral characters appear, they usually perform a dramatic function that relates somehow to the story overall. Peripheral characters may help the protagonist by explaining or presenting a necessary point of exposition, or they may hinder the protagonist by creating a barrier, literal or metaphorical. They may do both. In addition, peripheral characters will probably appear momentarily and may or may not speak to the protagonist, antagonist or secondary characters. They may be alone or in pairs or groups.

<u>IN A NUTSHELL:</u> A peripheral character is a minor character in your novel or screenplay who performs a story function, probably pertaining to the plot.

WHAT ARE PERIPHERAL CHARACTERS FOR?

Peripheral characters are essentially 'walk-on' parts in your narrative. If these peripheral characters speak, they most often orbit the protagonist (though not always). As with any characterisation, you don't want the addition of your peripherals to be entirely random! There has to be a point to them.

So, how can peripheral characters create problems for your protagonist? Well, in the case of authority figures, police may stop your protagonist at a checkpoint and want his or her ID; soldiers may be patrolling the perimeter of a place the hero wants to get into; or a doctor may treat a protagonist on the run, then call the cops. Receptionists, bartenders and other service providers may create other barriers or problems.

Occasionally, a peripheral character can help a protagonist: perhaps s/he gives your protagonist advice, or makes reference to something that brings your protagonist to an important realisation. You need to beware of using this device too obviously or neatly, otherwise it can seem like a contrivance. Wise tramps are completely overused in this way in spec scripts; I always ask in notes, 'When was the last time YOU met a homeless guy who just happened to give you the advice you needed at that moment?' However, random women DO talk to one another in public bathrooms and toilets and offer advice to one another, so this common trope still feels authentic.

Sometimes peripheral characters relate to the genre or type of story. We may see wave after wave of soldiers in war stories; plus, crowds frequently amass at airports, train and coach stations in disaster stories, to illustrate the extent of the problem facing the people affected. Alternatively, crowds may gather because of executions, pending apocalypses or alien invasions. In thrillers, more people seem to die in public toilets than they do in real life. Comedies involving student life may have more drunk and stoned partygoers than the average story, plus horrors will have more ghostly apparitions trying to pull characters into hell or beyond.

IN A NUTSHELL: Peripheral characters are most often additional, momentary obstacles or threats – especially for the protagonist – though occasionally these characters can help out, too. They are essentially plot devices, or thematic – or both.

WHO ARE PERIPHERAL CHARACTERS LIKELY TO BE?

In movies and television, peripheral characters are most often played by 'background artists', aka 'extras'. Some peripheral characters may have lines of dialogue, but these will usually be fleeting – perhaps one scene, usually less than a minute's worth of focus in the story. In novels, peripheral characters may appear more than this, especially in crime fiction and mystery as potential 'red herrings' or false leads; in other fiction they may provide a thematic function – as in family sagas, women's or literary fiction. Peripheral characters will vary in importance in scenes; the more focus there is on them individually, the more of a thematic or expositional function they provide in the story.

Examples of common peripheral characters in fiction, film and TV include:

- Gathering crowds
- Soldiers – especially on guard, on the battlefield or in the trenches, or similar
- Lynch mobs, mutinies and groups of vigilantes
- Newscasters, radio talk-show hosts, vloggers
- Police, doctor, teacher or other authority figure
- Receptionists, air stewards, bartenders or other members of the service industry
- Homeless people, especially tramps
- Additional monsters, vampires, zombies, ghosts, etc.
- Drunk and stoned people, especially at parties but also on the street

- People in public bathrooms and toilets (especially women)
- Random people causing a threat, nuisance or spectacle

Of course, not all stories have peripheral characters. In movies or TV with minimal casting, there may be none – especially in the case of the so-called 'contained' thriller or horror. Novels are most likely to have peripheral characters, but again this is not always the case.

IN A NUTSHELL: Peripheral characters are those characters who appear in the narrative in order to underline the point of the story in some way.

THEMES AND MESSAGES

The dictionary defines 'theme' as 'an idea that recurs in or pervades a work of art or literature', so it's not difficult to see how this pertains to novels, TV and film. Stories can essentially be about anything and, certainly, novelists', filmmakers' and creators' individual, specific messages can vary wildly. Also, because audiences are made up of individuals who are active participants in the story, how they perceive that message may also vary. At best, this can be an interesting and meaningful exchange between the creator and participant, either overtly between real people, or via the page and/or screen. At worst, this can be an awful addition to the relationship between creator and audience, either because the exchange becomes toxic or because it 'inspires' some sort of bad act. More on this in the next section.

IN A NUTSHELL: Audiences aren't passive and don't suck up everything writers and creators give them. How they decode and interpret various stories and characters – and the ideas within them – will depend on their worldviews and lived experiences.

MESSAGES AND 'RESPONSIBILITY'

What novelists and screenwriters are 'trying to say' is under greater scrutiny than ever in the social media age. Many writers are 'called out' for what some commentators believe are harmful or irresponsible messages in their work. Individual writers may be accused of inciting racial hatred; adding to rape culture; even of creating copy-cat crimes in the real world. One of the most famous, darkest misinterpretations of a work is The Beatles' White Album. The psychopathic murderer Charles Manson and his 'Family' of followers believed (mistakenly) The Beatles' songs on their iconic album were inciting violence and depictions of Armageddon. The killers daubed Beatles lyrics and slogans like 'Helter Skelter' in blood at their terrible crime scenes. Yet even if the White Album had incited these things, the notion Manson and his followers couldn't help but carry out the 'instructions' is absurd. They were grown adults who had been raised in a society whose pervading theme, message or idea is 'thou shalt not kill', after all. They made an active choice to go against this and commit murder.

<u>IN A NUTSHELL:</u> It's clear audiences are not passive participants, given the multiple interpretations of writers' work, whether 'right' or 'wrong' or somewhere in-between. So, the responsibility of the artiste can only be matched by the responsibility of the individual audience member (or those responsible for that audience member, i.e. parents or carers).

THEMES VERSUS STORYWORLD

In most storyworlds, our characters live in a reflection of the times in which we find ourselves as writers. Even in period drama and science fiction, our storyworlds – whether fiction, film or television – will be rooted in the various hierarchies we literally exist in now, with regard to:

- **Race.** The default of the Western, English-speaking world is white. We can see this everywhere, even down to the actual words 'ethnic minority' (according to the last census, the UK estimates roughly 13% of its population is BAME; the USA estimates approximately

23–38%, depending where you read the figures). Regardless of how you feel politically about this, the majority of stories incorporate white viewpoints and white people, whether current or historical. By this token, BAME culture is sidelined as a 'speciality' or 'niche' interest, the implication being whiteness is 'for everyone'. This element then adds to the current homogenisation of stories, so it's no wonder movies like *Moonlight* and *Hidden Figures* (both 2016) seem so fresh by comparison – we've literally been starved of stories of black LGBT people and period pieces starring black women!

BAME storyworlds in which many people of colour figure are usually religious or crime-related in terms of story. However, in the remake of Dean Craig's comedy *Death at a Funeral* (2007), the movie was remade in America in 2010 with a predominantly African-American cast... because why not? This didn't mean the US version was exactly the same as the UK version, either: 'The American humour and tone is different (to the British version),' says Craig, who had little input on the remake. 'The comedy is culturally specific. In the British version, it's all very much about what the secrets and lies mean to the family; it's embarrassing, awkward. In the US version, it's much more about the social implications of those revelations.'

IN A NUTSHELL: Watching remakes of the same movies and TV shows and listing how they differ culturally can be a real revelation in itself, even between two different English-speaking countries. Thanks to streaming and clips on YouTube, it's never been easier to check this out and see the contrasts.

• **Gender.** Feminism might have made considerable headway in the last ten years in particular, but we still live in a world of men. As a result, stories tend to be *about* (white) men more often, because women are still 'behind' historically. This means we are most likely to read or watch stories about white women, as this element intersects with race on this list. In comparison to 'minority ethnic', however, women make up 51% of the potential audience, meaning female-centric storyworlds are woefully underrepresented.

However, in certain genres and storyworlds, women are very much in charge – men may even be relegated to the supporting cast altogether. In novels, the romance and erotica genres may put the man in the role function occupied traditionally by the WAG (perhaps we could call it the Husband Or Boyfriend. HOB!). This may happen in the domestic noir subgenre of crime fiction, too. Occasionally movies will do this, such as *Premonition* (2007). While her husband's impending death is protagonist Linda's focus, she is surrounded by two daughters, a female best friend and her mother – almost unprecedented in a supernatural thriller film, where leads (male or female) may be isolated. Sometimes TV-show storyworlds are matriarchies, such as *The 100* (2014–present). There is no specific story reason for this, though it does contrast sharply with the more masculine order the Sky People previously had aboard the Ark in outer space.

IN A NUTSHELL: Sometimes placing the storyworld in a vastly different version of reality just means putting your female characters in charge of running it for once! This doesn't just mean female leads, but females in ALL the major and minor role functions, especially positions of power.

- **LGBT.** Society says most people are straight, aka heterosexual (the Office for National Statistics thinks the gay population is 1.5%, but some other estimates think the gay population could be as high as 10% in the UK). It's also thought most people are not transgender, with the current estimate of trans people in the UK at just 0.9%. Interestingly, this actually means the number of characters and stories about LGBT people is wildly out of whack with the actual figures if we're talking about democratic representation... but, LGBT characters and stories are disproportionately tragic or comedic.

IN A NUTSHELL: Even in coming-out or transition stories, LGBT characters tend to exist in isolation and rarely gather in large numbers. This seems strange, especially considering many LGBT-identifying people will band together for moral support, safety and, of course, fun!

- **Disability.** There are an incredible 6.9 million disabled people in the UK, according to the Disabled Living Foundation. This equates to 19% of the working population! It's a similar story in the USA, where the National Service Inclusion Project estimates approximately 48 million Americans are disabled (roughly 19% of the population again). So you can see why disabled activists call this group 'the largest minority' – they literally are. Yet where are the stories, characters and storyworlds that recognise this? As mentioned in the second part of this book, the *Mad Max* storyworld places disability at the heart of the narrative's storyworld. Otherwise, most disabled characters exist in a vacuum due to the 'Highlander Effect'.

  IN A NUTSHELL: There are very few stories in which disability forms part of the storyworld... yet it's a huge part of our world, nearly one in five people! So why not include the 'largest minority' – what could your story gain?

DISPOSABLE MEN

We've already discussed in part three of this book the notion of the 'Expendable Hero', an important secondary character in the action-adventure or thriller novel or movie (and occasionally TV). The audience tends to invest heavily in this character for a number of reasons, so there will be much wailing and gnashing of teeth when he dies. Expendable Hero is hardly ever a woman (white or black), and though, in the movie world, white actors may play him, it's most often a BAME actor, leading this trope to sometimes be called 'sacrificial minority'.

In comparison to Expendable Hero, then, there is a peripheral character whose primary function in the narrative is to die. I call him Disposable Man because we don't know anything about him other than what we see. He may be a soldier, a civilian or bystander; he may form part of the opposing force in a battle, or he may be on the protagonist's side; he may also be completely neutral. He may be killed by earthquakes, volcanoes, lightning, dinosaurs, aliens or zombies. He doesn't have a name and he won't even speak (though he may scream as he dies, usually horribly and flamboyantly). Instead, the reader or viewer is a voyeur: we meet this character in the moment of his death only.

Intriguingly, one thing I've noted over the years is how similar just about every Disposable Man peripheral character is, no matter the medium, novel or screenplay: they're nearly always young, white men in the region of 18 to 40 years old. I read a lot of dystopian, post-apocalyptic fiction, but even allowing for the notion I may be reading these peripheral characters as white automatically (being white myself), they're still always male. This is even more obvious in the film world, especially disaster movies. In a movie like *2012* (which predictably came out in 2012), a set piece like 'the dissolution of Los Angeles' shows the city torn apart, yet nearly every peripheral character killed is young, white and male! I suspect all this has more to do with the apparent fact most working stunt people are white and male, between the ages of 18 and 40, but there is a small yet significant contingent of female stunt people, and BAME ones as well, especially as some will double for stars who are also people of colour.

It's also worth remembering that disposable peripheral characters don't necessarily have to do anything especially dangerous – all they *really* need to do is die! One of the few franchises that kills off peripheral women at the same rate as men is *Resident Evil*. Overwhelmed by zombies, whether human or animal, there's no reprieve from being torn apart just because you're female! Peripheral characters who are BAME or teenagers don't tend to fare much better either (though small children are normally spirited away, presumably to be killed off-screen – another 'deal breaker' for audiences).

By the way, a bit of movie trivia for you: this tendency has found its way into cameos, too! Legendary Hollywood screenwriter and Spielberg collaborator David Koepp is listed as 'unlucky bastard' on the credits of his own movie *Jurassic Park: The Lost World* (1997) when he gets eaten by the T-Rex when it smashes on to the streets of San Diego.

IN A NUTSHELL: If you have peripheral characters in your novel or screenplay who need to die, if you want to be diverse, don't make them ALL default white male.

CROWDS

Crowds can be useful plot devices in fiction, film and TV and are not to be underestimated. Crowds are distinctly human and can create problems and solutions for the savvy writer's protagonist, such as moments of panic, mutiny or terror. We see this horrible side of human nature in *War of the Worlds* (2005) when a group of people hold our protagonist and his children up at gunpoint over his car. Crowds seem to be a particular interest of Steven Spielberg, as we see them crop up in many of his movies, not just those set in wartime. John Anderton in *Minority Report* (2002) not only loses son Sean in a crowded public pool, he uses crowds in the mall to 'lose' himself and Agatha, when he kidnaps the pre-cog from the tank. Jason Bourne does the same in crowded train stations and similar in the *Bourne* franchise.

But crowd scenes are expensive, with extras' fees to pay, not to mention health and safety considerations, so lower-budget film and television tend not to utilise them. But in a novel, there is of course no such budget constraint! Losing one's child is every parent's nightmare, so child-abduction novels have made a splash in recent years, probably because of high-profile, unsolved cases like that of Madeleine McCann. But with a subject so emotive, there are certain 'deal breakers' in place. In order for audiences to stay sympathetic to the protagonist's plight, it's important the reader doesn't blame the lead for losing the child in the first place (also illustrated by the case of Madeleine McCann, whose parents left her and her siblings alone).

This means crowds become useful in a child-abduction plot, because everyone in the audience understands children get lost in crowds very easily – it's probably happened to every parent, at least once. In *The Girl in the Red Coat* (2016) by Kate Hamer, eight-year-old Carmel is abducted from a crowded festival ground by a man claiming to be her grandfather. The panic of Carmel's mother, Beth, is beautifully captured as she first realises Carmel is missing and frantically searches tents, stalls and groups of children. A horrible sense of foreboding sets in as Beth hears the other searchers' calls for her daughter: there's no way her usually obedient, loving little girl would not come back at the sound of her own name. This is followed by Beth's refusal to leave the festival ground, in case Carmel comes back: she knows it makes no sense. Beth is adrift, alone, heartbroken – yet she is surrounded by people.

IN A NUTSHELL: Whether writing fiction, film or TV, a crowd scene can convey a number of emotions and/or obstacles relating to your protagonist. Use crowd scenes wisely, making them form a plot or character function. Don't stick them in for the sake of it.

ONLY 17%

While crowds in novels are frequently referred to as homogenised bodies, in crowd scenes in movies and television there is often a lack of diversity generally, too, especially with reference to the top four:

- **Race.** Most people in crowds are white. If a BAME character from the crowd appears, it's frequently a black man who may speak or carry out some sort of action that gets him killed or dragged off by a white authoritarian force. A notable exception would be TV's *Empire*, where neither of these things happens. The show has many scenes in Lucious Lyon's nightclub Leviticus, where black people party in the background as the main characters talk or do deals.

- **Gender.** Most people in crowds are male. According to the Geena Davis Institute on Gender in Media, just 17% of crowd scenes in movies and TV across the board include women. One movie that comes to my mind is the Oscar-winning *Argo* (2012), which – unusually – utilises Iranian female revolutionaries at the forefront of the crowds, though whether they make up more than 17% I have no idea (and I'm not counting frame by frame!).

- **LGBT.** Gay and transgender characters seem to suffer so much from what I call the 'Highlander Effect' that we very rarely see them gathering in movies and TV. Yet there's no reason they shouldn't: gay clubs, whether for dancing or cabaret – or both – are well entrenched on 'the scene', as illustrated by the likes of *Priscilla, Queen of the Desert* (1994) and *Flawless* (1999). In addition, Gay Pride and Trans Pride happen every year, worldwide. Yet there's only been one recent movie I can think of – *Pride* (2014) – that has large groups of LGBT people in the frame at any one time.

- **Disability.** Again, the 'Highlander Effect' comes into play, so we rarely see large groups of disabled people together in movies and on TV. When we do, it might be in a hospital or rehab setting, as in *Born on the Fourth of July* (1989). I can't think of a single show or movie in which disabled people gather in large groups for any other reason – nor could I find one in the course of my research – which is pretty shocking. The BBC1 idents, which feature a wheelchair-bound basketball team, was the best I could do! Oh, dear.

In addition, I would also add the following as lacking from crowd scenes:

- **Children and teenagers.** It's unsurprising kids are missing as standard from crowd scenes: children are expensive, as they need chaperones and tutors on set, plus they can only work certain hours by law (which, unhelpfully, can change according to which area you're filming in). In addition, it's not always appropriate for children to be present: you won't find kids in nightclubs, plus, in genres like horror, dead and mutilated children tend to turn even stalwart gore fans off. That said, you'll find children in crowd scenes in big-budget family movies, especially at school: the *Harry Potter* franchise is an obvious example, and *Paddington* (2014) made good use of schoolchildren, who, refreshingly, were ethnically diverse, too.

- **Old people.** The elderly seem to be missing from stories as standard – so the fact that they're missing from crowds, too, is completely predictable. If the leads are middle-aged or older, however, you're more likely to find elderly people in the crowds and background, as in the *Best Exotic Marigold Hotel* (2012–15) movies.

- **Animals.** Like children, animals are expensive, can only work certain hours, and bring with them many health and safety implications of their own. In TV and movies, animals and birds like eagles taking part in crowded battle scenes tend to be CGI – as we see in the *Lord of the Rings* and *Hobbit* franchises. If it's going to be that expensive, you might as well go the whole hog! However, if you're writing a novel, there's absolutely no reason you can't have animals in your crowd scenes. If it adds something to your story, why not?

Geena Davis's (@GDIGM) suggestion to help make crowd scenes in film more diverse as regards gender is simple, but effective:

> When describing a crowd scene, write in the script, 'A crowd gathers, which is half female.' That may seem weird, but I promise you, somehow or other on the set that day the crowd will turn out to be 17 percent female otherwise.

You could use this advice for ensuring there are more women in the crowd – or any other minority you like, in any medium. Obviously, you don't want to get sidetracked with too much description of the crowd – especially in a screenplay – but if you're going to use a crowd, make sure it's the most interesting it can be and pulls its weight story-wise.

<u>IN A NUTSHELL:</u> Think about WHO is in your crowd and why, in order for a crowd scene to work the best it can in your story, with relation to your protagonist.

SUMMING UP

✓ Peripheral characters can frequently create barriers or problems for main characters; they are rarely helpful, since this can seem a handy contrivance to the plot.

✓ Think about your walk-on peripheral characters who speak very carefully. What is their function?

✓ Peripheral characters are often thematic and relate to the message or point of the story in some way.

✓ Certain peripheral characters – like wise-prophet tramps – seem cheesy and overdone. Even a peripheral character must feel authentic, whether diverse or not.

✓ There is a homogenisation of peripheral characters, especially when we see lots of them (i.e. crowd scenes). Think about WHO is there and WHY.

✓ Most peripheral characters are white; most are males; hardly any are disabled or LGBT. Think about yours and how you can introduce diversity without letting your peripherals take up too much 'story space'.

✓ Think about how peripheral characters and what they're doing add to your plot and/or storyworld.

✓ In screenplays, crowd scenes are a budget issue and will often be cut; this is not the case in novels, for obvious reasons.

✓ In screenplays, peripheral characters are often played by background artistes or extras, or stunt men if they are supposed to die. Even if you are a novelist, thinking about who would have to BECOME that character can help you flesh it out, instead of creating cardboard cut-outs.

✓ Do your research by noting the peripheral characters in books, TV shows and movies. WHO are they? WHAT are they for?

✓ Many writers write peripheral characters into their novels and screenplays randomly, without thinking. Knowing WHAT peripheral characters are there for and what they signify will strengthen your writing and differentiate you from the average writer.

✓ Think about who is MISSING from the story.

LAST WORDS

'Part of the process of writing is not so much to explain your vision, but to discover it... You find out what you think.'

– Robert Towne

HOMOGENISATION = BORING

'There's a rule of writing: if everything is funny, nothing is funny; if everything is sad, nothing is sad. You need that contrast.' J. Michael Strazynski is the screenwriter of *Thor*, *World War Z* and the Oscar-winning *Changeling*. When he talks of contrast in writing, he makes a great point that is also relevant to diverse characters. In this book, we've already touched on the homogenised nature of characterisation across fiction, film and TV. Whether we look at heroes, villains or other archetypes or character tropes and role functions, they get stale and old quickly when they are overused. And they get overused in a risk-averse industry that is obviously not going to STOP doing something if it brings them a monetary return. Novels, films and TV are not education, but entertainment, after all.

The advent of the internet, especially social media, hasn't only given people unprecedented access to the creators of fiction, film and TV, but also means would-be consumers are now more media-literate than ever. This means various expected character tropes get old even faster. A call for more diverse, more differentiated characters has spread like wildfire online – but it's not just 'all talk'. Readers and audiences might have been saying this for years, but most excitingly, they are now putting their money where their mouths are and backing books, movies and TV shows in which characters and stories are more diverse than ever before.

IN A NUTSHELL: Rather than pass diversity off as a 'fad' or 'political correctness gone mad', the savvy writer recognises this offers new opportunities to grab untold stories and unusual characters with both hands and mine them to their full potential.

UNTOLD STORIES ARE POWERFUL

We live in a society that tends to present things a certain way all the time... and this includes storytelling. Sometimes it's obvious where we need diversity; other times it's not. Here's a short list of potential ways of looking at stories a different way, based on the commentary in this book:

- Period pieces that are NOT about slavery, but which focus on BAME characters?
- Biopics that place women at the centre (not Elizabeth I, or any other member of the royal family or aristocracy)?
- Dark stories about female murderers, serial killers, child abusers, human traffickers (true story and 'inspired by')?
- Lead characters who are derived from archetypes we don't often see in the protagonist's role – i.e. the Caregiver? The Magician?
- Female leads who don't need a relationship with a man, or a dead child?
- Heroes and sheroes who are gay or transgender?
- Villains whose motivations are scarily understandable and relevant, instead of outlandish and/or nonsensical?
- LGBT or disabled leads who solve crimes, go on dates, build or invent things?
- Single or young parents who are not abusive or negligent and good parents (without dying!)?

- Anti-heroes who are women, and/or BAME?
- Disabled characters who are not bitter or vulnerable, but capable members of the team who save the others?
- Storyworlds that 'invert' the usual white-centric, male-centric norms – what if there were mostly BAME people in charge? And/or women?
- Male leads who are emotionally literate and don't need 'saving' by a relationship with a woman? Or a man?

These are just starting points – and there are dozens more you can glean from this book, online and by talking to people in real life. Why not give it a try and unearth a few more?

IN A NUTSHELL: The key is not rehashing the same-old viewpoints and 'expected' characters, over and over. Mix things up, flip them, invert them, turn them upside down.

GET OUT OF YOUR COMFORT ZONE

While writers like to think they're rebels or 'left of the middle' thinkers, the reality is ALL of us are products of the environments, social norms and values we grow up with. It takes time, guts and effort to try and appreciate other people's points of view. It takes even more so to challenge our *own* assumptions and worldview, especially if we discover we are guilty of certain negative or prejudiced thoughts or feelings against a group of people.

I will give an – albeit uncomfortable – example of my own. In my teenage years and early twenties, I harboured many negative and prejudiced thoughts about fat people. While I never behaved outwardly like this towards people I knew, or in the street towards strangers, in my heart I felt fat people were disgusting and brought it all on themselves. Basically, I had absorbed society's diatribe against fat people wholesale, I'm ashamed to say. I've never been overweight myself, so it was quite odd I felt so strongly about this. I like to think I am a sympathetic and understanding person overall, yet this was a complete empathy fail!

So, I put it under the microscope and found, to my immense surprise, that my prejudice was *not really about* fat people. I'd had an eating disorder as a teen and it followed me into my twenties. Every time I saw a fat person, I felt a combination of fear, shame and anger, not at them, but *myself*... which I then pushed outwards, at those 'faceless' fat people. My behaviour was the epitome of that old adage you may see on Facebook memes: 'People don't do things because of you. They do things because of themselves.'

IN A NUTSHELL: The uncomfortable reality is, however liberal we are, every one of us has prejudices. Knowing what ours are means we're able to deal with them. It also offers a fantastic opportunity to nail a diverse character, because if you find yourself in the grip of such thoughts, others will undoubtedly feel the same. Use your own prejudices as a starting point for cracking open a diverse character and bringing authenticity and understanding to your story.

VARIETY IS KEY

In recent years, many furores have hit the headlines, especially on social media, when it comes to diverse characterisation. This is magnified tenfold when we consider the hotly debated tropes BAME, female, LGBT and disabled characters frequently fall into, especially as secondary characters. Writers, filmmakers and creators have been asked to consider various characterisation ideals, tests and pledges like the Bechdel Test, or even flat out TOLD they 'shouldn't' use a particular trope, and if they do, they're bad people! There have been arguments, accusations and full-on skirmishes (some deserved, some not so much) and, yet again, it's been proved the road to hell really DOES start with good intentions.

Yet we rarely see such skirmishes focused on white male characterisation generally, which I always find very interesting. I think this is most likely because for every BAD white male character – and there are, of course, many, many of these – there are just as many, if not more, great white male characters who speak to readers and audiences. Look at any 'best of' movie lists and you'll probably find the vast majority have white male leads. A recent list published by the British Film Institute (BFI) backs this up (as if evidence were needed!): only *Tokyo Story* (1953) and *The Passion of Joan of Arc* (1927) are the exceptions in their top ten. The website 'Greatest Books' (www.greatestbooks.org) is generated from a whopping 114 different sources and has a similar, male-centric top ten at the time of writing, with only *Madame Bovary* by Gustave Flaubert at number ten boasting a female protagonist.

So, rather than demanding writers, filmmakers and creators write diverse characters in specific ways, or actively stop them from attempting various tropes, I would argue what diverse characterisation needs is MORE of what we're doing right now! Flood the market with diverse characters, just as we've been flooded with white male characters all these years. While it's true some of those new diverse characters will be duds, others will be neutral and some will be fantastic; it will all balance out in the end. In real terms, diversity is about having more variety. Nothing more; nothing less.

'I don't think diversity is "just" about putting a woman, BAME, LGBT into a tired old trope,' says Gail Hackston, a writer/director who is herself gay. 'I think our responsibility as writers and indeed creators – because this goes to directors, casting agents and producers, too – is to go beyond the trope full stop. That includes ensuring we think through every aspect of the character and look beyond what our own worlds look like. Diversity in look and in feel.'

IN A NUTSHELL: Don't think 'diversity', think VARIETY. Put unusual characters in situations and stories we don't expect, but make them authentic and relevant.

ADD TO THE PICTURE, DON'T TAKE FROM IT

It's a sad fact that diverse characters are under greater scrutiny – but this is because people are so desperate to see something they recognise, not necessarily just from their own lives, but also something that feels fresh, relevant and relatable.

No one writer carries the responsibility for ALL characterisation or tropes on his/her shoulders, no matter what Twitter might say. It's a cumulative build-up and we can only contribute. It's unlikely any writer sets out to overtly oppress anyone in his or her work: mistakes may be made, but it's also worth remembering that, when it comes to characterisation and storytelling generally, there is no ideal or agreed 'best'. One wo/man's meat is another's poison and creators mustn't forget that. No story is for 'everyone', not even the most successful for mass audiences!

Buzzwords, agendas, hashtags, tests and pledges, academia, fan fiction, good intentions... none of it will provide readers and audiences with what they really want, which is simply 'a good story well told'. If you can do this, as a novelist or screenwriter, this in turn gives the industry what it wants, which is lots of sales! Research is key in creating an authentic character and story – the worst thing writers can do is simply copy from existing stories. Storytelling provides an invaluable function in helping us decode and relate to the world around us, but at the same time, it's not education or outreach work, it's entertainment... and people find it entertaining to see reflections of themselves, their lives, struggles or even just their abstract feelings in a work! This is why it's so difficult to separate one from the other and why what 'good' representation is will ultimately go round in circles.

Don't forget: this issue will be in constant flux. You will never catch up and you simply cannot please everyone. Instead, do the best you can for your character and story, and research it well. Never copy directly from what you see in other stories, but rather, find your own truth. If it's relevant to you, it will be relatable to others. Don't worry about the 'responsibility of the artiste' or what people might say. Instead, be rounded, open and fair in your own interests... and the rest should take care of itself.

'Writers have a responsibility to tell the best stories we can,' says crime novelist Sarah Hilary, author of the DI Marnie Rome series. 'If we read widely (as all writers should) and keep ourselves in the world (as all writers should) then we ought, with the aid of our empathy and imagination, to be able to create believable characters of every colour, race and creed. Every story we tell should be attuned to the world we're writing about and sensitive to its pain, its pleasure, its struggles. If we fulfil these obligations then I feel we've done all we can.'

If variety is the key, then great diverse characterisation comes from being 'left of the middle', rather than 'out of the left field'. If we've had more diverse secondary characters, now is the time to flip the expected white leads and show more BAME people in the protagonist's and antagonist's roles; or show LGBT, disabled or female characters in role functions we don't expect, within storylines and genres where they don't usually appear. We also need to remember these groups are not the only marginalised ones in general storytelling, plus they can intersect as well, as demonstrated by the recent critical acclaim lavished on the book and movie of *Hidden Figures*, as well as its considerable commercial success. Readers and audiences showed up for this tale of black female excellence, not because the characters were BAME, or because they were female. It's a familiar story – we've heard and seen many NASA stories with white men at the helm – but, in a world where readers and audiences are beginning to tire of familiar stories, this one felt fresh and relevant. The book and film succeeded not because of novelty value, or because of 'political correctness gone mad', either. The last word for this book has to go to *Hidden Figures*' author, Margot Lee Shetterly, who nails it when she says: 'It's a great story... and that alone makes it worth telling.'

IN A NUTSHELL: Find your great story, worth telling... and challenge yourself to find a new way of looking at it. This is the way you will bring forth a great diverse character who readers and/or audiences will respond to.

So, there we have it! Good luck!

RESOURCES

Number-crunching can illustrate gaps in the market and help us find our target audiences; plus, reading about the rich tapestry of human experiences and endeavours can help feed our own ideas. But when it comes to actually writing diverse characters and stories, nothing beats talking to REAL, actual people!

Here are some things to consider when tracking down people and their stories, whether you're writing a biography, or researching a particular diverse character and/or time period, or something else.

ON RESEARCH

Many writers mistakenly believe research is 'only' about reading articles, blogs and books on craft. In real terms it's much more than this – and much more organic. The savvy writer is constantly researching, looking for new ideas and perspectives wherever s/he goes:

- **Read and visit local.** Lots of writers are so global-focused, they miss what's right under their noses. Yet the history of your own area is rich and varied, with plenty of potential for storytelling – plus it means you'll be able to find real people to talk to very easily. In addition, reading local newspapers, visiting local museums and relating the history of your area to your own experiences could open up any number of ideas for characters and storylines. When I visited the museum of Lynmouth – just two small rooms – I saw a small display about how the tiny seaside village had been at the forefront of hydro-electric power in Victorian times. Though I knew Lynmouth well having visited since I was a child, I'd never realised such a small place could have such historical significance. From this new knowledge, my dystopian novella *Skyjack* (2016) grew.

- **Interviews can really help 'inform' characters.** Talking to real people who've had to face certain world or life events, adverse or not, is key in ensuring a character feels relatable, relevant and authentic. Characters tend to feel flat and lifeless at best if you depend on what you've seen on-screen and read already; at worst, they can feel tropey and derivative. Keep your characters fresh by interviewing real people and you will find all kinds of opinions and ideas that would never have occurred to you on your own. Two (or more) heads really are better than one!

- **Identifying characters and stories 'like' yours.** Too many writers avoid reading books or watching movies and TV shows like their own because they 'don't want to be influenced' by their predecessors. Ironically, this means it's far more likely they're destined to repeat what has gone before! The only way a writer can break new ground is by steeping him/herself in previous stories and characters. So, stop trying to avoid the work and identify which properties tread similar ground to yours, then read/watch everything you can.

- **Get out of your comfort zone.** I've written a lot on my blog about 'why this story?' – the question producers and publishers may ask you, in relation to why this is a story that MUST be told. I also believe writers should add 'why this character?' to the mix, justifying what it is that makes our chosen characters' worldviews so compelling. Asking ourselves if our characters or storyworlds include not only the good or neutral elements of race, gender, LGBT or disability, but the BAD things as well, can aid the potential conflict of the story. It's not always nice to think of these bad things – we don't want to put our characters through it! – but it's necessary if we're going to tell the best story possible. Drama is conflict, after all!

RESEARCH ONLINE

The good news is, thanks to the web, it's easier than ever to find people whose stories and worldviews we're interested in. BUT STOP RIGHT THERE. While there is no 'right' way to approach people whose worldviews and experiences you're interested in, there are multiple pitfalls you can fall into. Chew these over before you bombard strangers with questions:

- **Crowdsourcing.** One of the easiest and most productive ways of getting people to answer your questions or share their opinions is by 'putting it out there' online, rather than actively pursuing others. Facebook is particularly useful for this, as friends will be able to judge your sincerity against your previous statuses; your photos, interests, etc. Writers also tend to band together on Facebook, too, which means they generally have lots of friends and you have more likelihood of finding people willing to answer your query. Twitter is one of my favourite platforms for finding marginalised groups. 'Black Twitter' and 'Asian Twitter' are very lively on there – if you Google terms like 'top Black Twitter accounts' you will find interesting people to follow. There is a strong but significant contingent of gay and trans activists on there, too, as well as disability advocates. Reddit has some interesting threads and conversations, but does have a tendency to start flame wars and even storms of trolling very easily, so if you're of a delicate disposition I would recommend staying away! Another site that is particularly useful is www.quora.com. For the uninitiated, this a question and answer site where people can share their thoughts, experiences, judgements, values and more on every topic you can imagine. I've crowdsourced all kinds of answers on Quora, including what it's like to be in a house fire; people's experiences of single parenthood; what it feels like to have an eating disorder; or to experience bullying. I've also answered many questions, too.

IN OTHER WORDS: Use Facebook to find interesting people's opinions; Twitter and Quora are also particularly useful.

- **Watch out for broadcasters.** As mentioned in the market research section of this book in part one, some people on platforms like Twitter and Facebook are broadcasting their views, which means they are less likely to be open to questions and/or conversations. The reasons for broadcasting can vary wildly and don't mean the person is necessarily hostile; they could have limited time and/or brainspace, especially if they are frequently targeted by trolls. Other accounts are LITERAL broadcasts and have been prepared in advance and automated via Hootsuite or similar... so you won't get a reply, because there's no one there!!

  IN OTHER WORDS: Find out a person's remit first, *before* trying to engage them in conversation.

- **Don't start with questions.** Unless someone online invites questions – like I do, via @Bang2write – never steam into a thread with someone you don't know with questions on potentially incendiary topics like race, gender, sexuality, etc. Remember, the internet is remote communication, so it may not be apparent what your motive is. Also, marginalised people, especially women and/or people of colour, get hassle daily online simply for expressing their views. This means, rightly or wrongly, they may believe a sudden or baldly stated question is an act of aggression, even if it's not. Follow marginalised people; read their TLs and retweet them, engaging with them in discussion first, THEN ask them questions another day – you're much more likely to open a healthy and productive dialogue.

  IN OTHER WORDS: Don't make a question your <u>first</u> communication.

- **Watch out for flamers.** Some people say they want to discuss issues like diversity in fiction, film and TV, when in reality all they want is a ruck. These people are pretty obvious, as they tend to jump all over various articles on the subject they're talking about. They're the type to say writers are bad people and use continually negative language to describe media output, especially

Hollywood's, but particularly stories involving female leads who are apparently 'all' rubbish (even if they're female themselves!). This is where checking out timelines in advance can really work out as you will spot persistent naysayers very easily.

<u>IN OTHER WORDS:</u> Stay away from these people. Life is too short!

- **Go to organisations and authorities in the community first.** If you're finding it difficult to source people's opinions and experiences, or need a large number of people's answers, or worry about running into flamers or similar, a great short cut is to target organisations and authority figures in the communities you are interested in. Identify organisations via Google and follow them on social media, so you can discover if they hold any specific chats or Q&A sessions. Requests for RTs can work, too, with some. If you're looking for individuals, try Google for lists of influential Twitter accounts, or use related hashtags and key words. Activists and advocates make themselves easy to find, but do remember they can be vulnerable to abuse and harassment so may not reply to people they don't know and/or follow back. If you don't get a response, don't take it personally – just move on and try someone else.

TO READ MORE ABOUT DIVERSITY ONLINE

This is by no means a complete list, and new voices crop up all the time – so please pardon me if your favourite is not included. Think of this list as a 'starter pack' for writers interested in diversity across the 'top four' categories I mention in this book.

- **The Media, Diversity and Social Change Initiative**
  http://annenberg.usc.edu/pages/DrStacyLSmithMDSCI
  @MDSCInitiative

- **The Critical Media Project**
  http://www.criticalmediaproject.org / @critmedpro

- **Hollywood Diversified**
  http://diversifyhollywood.org / @diversifyhwood

- **Media Diversified**
  www.mediadiversified.org / @WritersOfColour

- **The Geena Davis Institute on Gender in Media** – See Jane
  http://www.seejane.org / @GDIGM

- **Go into the Story**
  https://gointothestory.blcklst.com / @GoIntoTheStory

- **Jane Friedman**
  https://janefriedman.com / @JaneFriedman

- **Women Writers**
  http://www.booksbywomen.org / @WomenWriters

- **Women in Film and Television (UK)**
  https://wftv.org.uk / @WFTV_UK
  plus Women in Film and Television International
  http://www.wifti.net

- **Women in Film, TV, Media, Digital**
  https://womeninfilm.org/ffi/

- **The Gay and Lesbian Alliance Against Defamation** – GLAAD
  http://www.glaad.org / @glaad

- **LGBT Foundation**
  http://lgbt.foundation / @LGBTfdn

- **Diversability**
  http://www.mydiversability.com / @diversability

- **Everyday Ableism**
  http://everydayableism.weebly.com / @EAbleism

In addition, make sure you check out who is writing/making what, plus the loglines and pitches of each project. It's easy to keep up to date with this now – follow and subscribe to *Variety*, the *Hollywood*

Reporter, *The Bookseller*, *IMDBPro*, *Box Office Mojo*, the BFI, the Oscars, BAFTA, *Deadline*, *Done Deal Pro*, even *Buzzfeed*... but you're doing all this already, right??

DON'T FORGET!

There is now a Facebook group for interested writers, called Bang2writers. It's a lively, diverse group of writers from numerous backgrounds at varying stages of their careers; there are also some filmmakers, authors and even a few literary agents in there, too. Simply search for it, or use URL www.facebook.com/groups/Bang2writers.

My site at www.bang2write.com now has a 'diversity' label under 'categories' on the right-hand sidebar of the site if you're using the desktop version. If you're on a phone, the easiest thing to do to find relevant articles is Google 'Bang2write diversity' and you'll find them all.

Articles focus on characterisation and untold stories, as well as intentional inclusion of marginalised characters, writers, filmmakers and authors. If you would like to write an article, please do check out the submission details at: www.bang2write.com/write-for-b2w.

ONE LAST THING, LIEUTENANT (OKAY, MAYBE TWO...)

To sign off, a great philosopher once said:

'Our similarities make us strong. Our differences make us stronger.'

Okay, it was the 2009 winners of *Britain's Got Talent*, dance troupe Diversity. Seems fitting though – and true!!

About Us

In addition to Creative Essentials, Oldcastle Books has a number of other imprints, including No Exit Press, Kamera Books, Pulp! The Classics, Pocket Essentials and High Stakes Publishing
> oldcastlebooks.co.uk

Checkout the kamera film salon for independent, arthouse and world cinema **> kamera.co.uk**

For more information, media enquiries and review copies please contact Clare **> marketing@oldcastlebooks.com**